The World as Dream

Other books from the same Author.

1. **Dharma, The Categorial Imperative**; edited by Ashok Vohara, Arvind Sharma and Mrinal Miri; ISBN 81-246-0270-0
2. **A New Curve in the Ganges** — Mahatma Gandhi's Interpretation of Hinduism; by Arvind Sharma; ISBN 81-246-0271-9
3. **New Focus on Hindu Studies**; by Arvind Sharma; ISBN 81-246-0307-3
4. **Sea-shell as Silver** — A Metaphorial Excursion into Advaita Vedānta; by Arvind Sharma; ISBN 81-246-0352-9
5. **The World as Image**; by Arvind Sharma; ISBN 81-246-0362-6

The World as Dream

Arvind Sharma
McGill University

D.K. Printworld (P) Ltd.
New Delhi

Cataloging in Publication Data — DK
[Courtesy: D.K. Agencies (P) Ltd. <docinfo@dkagencies.com>]

Sharma, Arvind, 1940–
The world as dream / Arvind Sharma.
vii, 222 p. 23 cm.
Includes bibliographical references (p.)
Includes indexes.
ISBN 8124603650

1. Dreams — Religious aspects. 2. Metaphor — Religious aspects. 3. Advaita. 4. Vedanta. 5. Philosophy, Hindu. I. Title.

DDC 181.4 22

ISBN 81-246-0365-0
First published in India in 2006

Published and printed by:
D.K. Printworld (P) Ltd.
Regd. Office: 'Sri Kunj', F-52, Bali Nagar
New Delhi-110 015
Phones: (011) 2545-3975; 2546-6019; *Fax*: (011) 2546-5926
E-mail: dkprintworld@vsnl.net
Website: www.dkprintworld.com

Preface

ADVAITA Vedānta may be described as a form of philosophical idealism, inasmuch as it looks upon the world as an immaterial phenomenon rather than as a physical object. So a heavy object, according to this view, would be no more than a dense thought. In fact the approach is rarefied even further in Advaita Vedānta and the world is often accorded the status of a dream.

This book constitutes an exploration of this marked tendency in Advaita Vedānta to conceive of the world as a dream, and incorporates the role played by dreams in other cultures, as well as recent advances in the scientific study of dreams, for the light they shed on the perception of the world as dream in Advaita Vedānta.

Contents

1

The World as Dream
An Introduction

THE rope-snake metaphor is more or less particular to the Advaita Vedānta school of Hindu philosophy but the dream-metaphor is more universal in character. What is characteristic about it is not so much its *presence* as its *use* in Advaita. But one may first testify to its widespread usage before exploring its use in Advaita.

The "world as dream" is a thread which runs through several cultures. Joseph Campbell has strung together the following sayings from different cultures to exemplify this point.[1]

> We are such stuff/As dreams are made of,
> And our little life/Is rounded with a sleep.
>
> — Shakespeare, "The Tempest"
>
> There is a dream dreaming us.
>
> — A Kalahari Bushman

The Chinese sage, Chuang-Tzu, dreamt he was a butterfly and on waking wondered whether, if he had then been a man dreaming a butterfly, might it not now be a butterfly dreaming it was a man.

---

1. Joseph Campbell, *The Mythic Image*, Princeton: Princeton University Press, 1974, p. 1.

That we come to this earth to live is untrue:
We come but to sleep, to dream.

— Aztec poem, Anonymous

La Vida es Sueno: "A Life is a Dream"

— Title of a play by Calderon

These parallels pertaining to the imagery of world as dream are striking, even exciting. Let us pursue, for instance, the famous anecdote already alluded to about Chuang-Tzu, who was also known as Chuang Chou.[2] Once upon a time he dreamed that "he was a butterfly, a butterfly fluttering about, enjoying itself. It did not know that is was Chuang Chou. Suddenly he awoke with a start and he was Chuang Chou again. But he did not know whether he was Chuang Chou who had dreamt that he was a butterfly, or whether he was a butterfly dreaming that he was Chuang Chou."[3] This role-reversal which puzzled Chuang-Tzu has a parallel from India. King Janaka is said to have had a dream upon waking from which he asked his guru: "Am I a king dreaming of being a beggar or a beggar dreaming of being a king?" A popular parable of Hinduism also employs the dream metaphor in a similar vein:

> A son was born to a king. He was the only child and was therefore "the apple of the eye" of both the king and the queen. The prince became a favourite with all and as he grew older he was taught all the arts and the sciences. One day, all of a sudden, the prince fell ill. The malady went on getting worse and even the best physician of the kingdom found that all treatments were of no avail. Both the king and the queen never left his

---

2. Wm. Theodore de Bary *et al.*, *Sources of Chinese Tradition,* New York: Columbia University Press, 1960, Volume I, p. 73.
3. Maurice Frydman, tr., *I am That: Conversations with Sri Nisargadatta Maharaj,* Bombay (Mumbai): Chetana, 1973, Part I, p. 263.

side day and night and the most competent physician and nurses continuously attended on him. The king was exhausted by his constant vigil and one night he could not resist falling asleep. He was awakened by the sound of crying and weeping and learned that the prince had passed away while he was asleep. The king sat as if he was stupefied, without speaking a single word. The queen asked him how it was that on the passing away of the only child whom he loved so much there was not a single drop of tear in his eyes. The king said, "Oh queen, when I fell asleep I dreamed that I had become the monarch of a large kingdom, much larger than mine, and the father of the seven worthy and ideal princes each of whom was well trained in the art of administration. I handed over the charge of my kingdom to them and thereafter I was spending my days in peace and happiness with you. And now this tragedy has taken place and I am unable to make up my mind whether I should lament for the child that has left us today or whether I should mourn the loss of the seven sons and a vast kingdom. I see no difference in the two bereavements and to me the world has become nothing but a dream."[4]

Chuang-Tzu himself elsewhere elaborates the idea of "world as dream" as follows:

How do I know that the love of life is not a delusion? How do I know that he who is afraid of death is not like a man who left his home as a youth and forgot to return? Lady Li was the daughter of the border warden of Ai. When she was first brought to the state of Chin, she wept until the bosom of her robe was drenched with tears. But when she came to the royal residence, shared with the king his luxurious couch and ate sumptuous food, she regretted that she had wept. How do I

4. Swami Sambuddhānanda, *Vedanta Through Stories*, Bombay (Mumbai): Sri Ramakrishna Ashram, 1959, pp. 44-45.

> know that the dead do not repent of their former craving for life? Those who dream of a merry drinking party may the next morning wail and weep. Those who dream, they may even try to interpret their dream. Only when they have awakened do they begin to know that they have dreamed. By and by comes the great awakening, and then we shall know that it has all been a great dream. Yet all the while the fools think that they are awake; this they are sure of. With minute nicety, they discriminate between princes and grooms. How stupid! Confucius and you are both in a dream. This way of talking may be called paradoxical. If after ten thousand generations we could once meet a great sage who knew how to explain the paradox, it would be as though we met him after only one morning or one evening.[5]

The way the idea of the "world as dream" may generate the time-warp Chuang-Tzu refers to at the end of the passage is illustrated by the experience of Mahāsena as recounted in the *Tripurā-Rahasya*. In the holy town Sundara in the country of Vaṅga reigned the King Susena. He has a brother named Mahāsena. To commemorate his long and prosperous rule, King Susena decided to perform the horse-sacrifice. As a part of the ritual, the horse roams around the country as symbolic of the king's paramountcy and is sacrificed in the end. Its movements must be unhindered, otherwise it is construed as a challenge to royal authority. Mahāsena, the brother of Susena, followed the horse along with the army. When they reached the banks of the Irrawaddy, however, the elated princes passed by a royal sage without saluting him. His son witnessed the insult and made the horse disappear, and decimated the army. Mahāsena returned to his brother with the news of the mishap and the king,

5. See Wm. Theodore de Bary *et al.*, *Sources of Chinese Tradition*, Part I, p. 72.

divining the reasons for the catastrophe, asked his brother to return to the spot and make amends for the oversight in sacred courtesy. This pleased the son of the sage who had carried away the horse. It was now returned but Mahāsena was baffled as to how the sage's son could have concealed the horse and the army in a small hill. To satisfy his curiosity, the sage's son took Mahāsena on a circuit of the hill through yogic powers. By the time Mahāsena returned, however, aeons had elapsed. Mahāsena found the whole world changed. The people, the river courses, the trees, the tanks, etc., were all different. He was bewildered and asked the saint:

"Oh great one! How long have we spent seeing your world? This world looks different from the one I was accustomed to!" Thus asked, the sage's son said to Mahāsena: "Listen King, this is the world which we were in and left to see that within the hill. The same has undergone enormous changes owing to the long interval of time. We spent only one day looking round the hill region: the same interval counts for twelve thousand years in this land; and it has accordingly changed enormously. Look at the difference in the manners of the people and their languages. Such changes are natural. I have often noticed similar changes before.

"Look here! This is the Lord, my father in samādhi. Here you stood before, praising my father and praying to him. There you see the hill in front of you.

"By this time, your brother's progeny has increased to thousands. What was Vaṅga, your country, with Sundara, your capital, is now a jungle infested with jackals and wild animals. There is now one Vīrabāhu in your brother's line who has his capital Viśāla on the banks of the Kṣiprā in the country of Mālwā; in your line, there is Suśarmā, whose capital is Vardhana in the country of the Draviḍas, on the banks of the

Tāmbraparṇī. Such is the course of the world which cannot remain the same even for a short time. For in this period, the hills, rivers, lakes, and the contours of the earth have altered. Mountains subside; plains heave high; deserts become fertile; plateaus change to sandy tracts; rocks decompose and become silt; clay hardens sometimes; cultivated farms become barren and barren lands are brought under tillage; precious stones become valueless and trinkets become invaluable; salt water becomes sweet and potable waters become brackish; some lands contain more people than cattle, others are infested with wild beasts; and yet others are invaded by venomous reptiles, insects and vermin. Such are some of the changes that happen on the earth in the course of time. But there is no doubt that this is the same earth as we were in before."

Mahāsena heard all that the sage's son said and fainted from the shock. Then being brought round by his companion, he was overcome by grief and mourned the loss of his royal brother and brother's son and of his own wife and children. After a short time, the sage's son assuaged his grief with wise words: "Being a sensible man, why do you mourn and at whose loss? A sensible man never does anything without a purpose; to act without discernment is childish. Think now, and tell me what loss grieves you and what purpose your grief will serve."

Asked thus, Mahāsena, who was still inconsolable, retorted: "Great sage that you are, can you not understand the cause of my sorrow? How is it that you seek the reason of my grief when I have lost my all? A man is generally sad when only one of his family dies. I have lost all my friends and relatives and you still ask me why I am sad."

The sage's son continued derisively. "King! Tell me now. Is this lapse into sorrow a hereditary virtue? Will it result in sin if you do not indulge in it on this occasion? Or, do you hope to recover your loss by such grief? King! Think well and tell me what you gain by your sorrow. If you consider it irresistible, listen to what I say.

"Such loss is not fresh. Your forefathers have died before. Have you ever mourned their loss? If you say that it is because of blood relationship that it now causes you grief, were there not worms in the bodies of your parents, living on their nourishment? Why are they not your relatives and why does not their loss cause you sorrow? King, think! Who are you? Whose deaths are the cause of your present grief?

"Are you the body, or other than that? The body is simply a conglomerate of different substances. Harm to any one of the constituents is harm to the whole. There is no moment in which each of the components is not changing. But the excretions do not constitute a loss to the body.

"Those whom you called your brother and so on are mere bodies; the bodies are composed of earth; when lost, they return to earth; and earth resolves ultimately into energy. Where then is the loss?

"In fact you are not the body. You own the body and call it your own, just as you do a garment you happen to possess. Wherein lies the difference between your body and your garment? Have you any doubt regarding this conclusion? Being other than your own body, what relation is there between you and another body? Did you ever claim similar relationship, say with your brother's clothes? Why then mourn over the loss of bodies, which are in no way different from garments?

"You speak of "my" body, "my" eyes, "my" life, "my" mind and so on, I ask you now to tell me what precisely you are."

Being confronted thus, Mahāsena began to think over the matter, and unable to solve the problem, he asked leave to consider it carefully. Then he returned and said with all humility "Lord, I do not see who I am. I have considered the matter, and still I do not understand. My grief is only natural; I cannot account for it.

"Master, I seek your protection. Kindly tell me what it is. Everyone is overpowered by grief when his relative dies. No one seems to know his own self; nor does one mourn all losses.

"I submit to you as your disciple. Please elucidate this matter to me."

Being thus requested, the sage's son spoke to Mahāsena: "King, listen! People are deluded by the illusion cast by Her Divine Majesty. They partake of misery that is due to the ignorance of their selves. Their misery is meaningless.

"As long as the ignorance of the self lasts, so long will there be misery.

"Just as a dreamer is foolishly alarmed at his own dreams or as a fool is deluded by the serpents created in a magic performance, so also is the man ignorant as the Self terrified.

"Just as the dreamer awakened from his fearful dream, or the man attending the magic performance informed of the unreal nature of the magic creations, no longer fears them but ridicules another who does, so also one aware of the Self not only does not grieve but also laughs at another's grief. Therefore, O valiant hero, batter down this impregnable fortress of illusion and conquer your misery by realization of the Self. In the meantime, be discriminating and not so foolish."

After hearing the sage's son, Mahāsena said, "Master, your illustration is not to the point. Dream or magic is later realised to be illusory whereas this hard concrete universe is always real and purposeful. This is unassailed and persistent. How can it be compared to the evanescent dream?" The sage's son answered: "Listen to what I say. Your opinion that the illustration is not to the point is a *double delusion like a dream in a dream*.[6]

"Consider the dream as a dreamer would, and tell me whether the trees do not afford shade to the pedestrians, and bear fruits for the use of others. Is the dream realised to be untrue and evanescent in the dream itself?

"Do you mean to say that the dream is rendered false after waking from it? Is not the waking world similarly rendered false in your dream or deep sleep?

"Do you contend that the waking state is not so because there is continuity in it after you wake up? Is there no *continuity in your dreams from day to day*?

"If you say that it is not evident, tell me whether the continuity in the wakeful world is not broken up every moment of your life.

"Do you suggest that the hills, the seas and the earth itself are really permanent phenomena, in spite of the fact that their appearance is constantly changing? Is not the dream-world also similarly continuous with its earth, mountains, rivers, friends and relatives?

"Do you still doubt its abiding nature? Then extend the same reasoning to the nature of the wakeful world and know it to be equally evanescent.

---

6. Note: - The commentary says that the first delusion is the idea of separateness of the universe from oneself and that the second is the idea that dream objects are an illusion in contradistinction to those seen while awake. This is compared to the illusion that *a dreamer mistakes the dream-rope for a dream-serpent*. (The dream is itself an illusion and the mistake is an illusion in the illusion.)

"The ever-changing objects like the body, trees, rivers, and islands are easily found to be transitory. Even mountains are not immutable, for their contours change owing to the erosion of waterfalls and mountain torrents, ravages by men, boars and wild animals, insects, thunder, lightning and storms, and so on. You will observe similar change in the seas and on earth.

"Therefore, I tell you that you should investigate the matter closely. (You will probably argue as follows:)

"Dream and wakefulness resemble each other in their discontinuous harmony (like a chain made up of links). There is no unbroken continuity in any object because every new appearance implies a later disappearance. But continuity cannot be denied in the fundamentals underlying the objects!

"Because a dream creation is obliterated and rendered false by present experience — what distinction will you draw between the fundamentals underlying the dream objects and the present objects?

"If you say that the dream is an illusion and its fundamentals are equally so, whereas the present creation is not so obliterated and its fundamentals must therefore be true, I ask you what illusion is. It is determined by the transitory nature, which is nothing but appearance to, and disappearance from, our senses.

"Is not everything obliterated in deep sleep? If you maintain, however, that mutual contradiction is unreliable as evidence and so proves nothing, it amounts to saying that self-evident sight alone furnishes the best proof. Quite so; people like you do not have a true insight into the nature of things.

"Therefore, take my word for it, the present world is only similar to the dream world. Long periods pass in dreams also. Therefore, purposefulness and enduring nature are in every way similar to both states. Just as you are obviously aware in your waking state, so also you are in your dream state.

"These two states being so similar, why do you not mourn the loss of your dream relations?

"The wakeful universe appears so real to all only by force of habit. If the same be imagined vacuous, it will melt away into the void.

"One starts imagining something; then contemplates it; and by continuous or repeated association resolves that it is true unless contradicted. In that way, the world appears real in the manner one is used to it. My world that you visited furnishes the proof thereof; come now, let us go round the hill and see."

Saying so, the sage's son took the King, and went round the hill and returned to the former spot.

Then he continued: "Look, O King! The circuit of the hill is hardly two miles and a half and yet you have seen a universe within it. Is it real or false? Is it a dream or otherwise? What has passed as a day in that land, has counted for twelve thousand years here; which is correct? Think, and tell me. Obviously, you cannot distinguish this from a dream and cannot help concluding that the world is nothing but imagination. My world will disappear instantly if I cease contemplating it.

"Therefore, convince yourself of the dream-like nature of the world and do not indulge in grief at your brother's death.

"Just as the dream creations are pictures moving on the mind screens, so also this world including yourself is the obverse of the picture depicted by pure intelligence and it is nothing more than an image in a mirror. See how you will feel after this conviction. Will you be elated by the accession of a dominion or depressed by the death of a relative in your dream?

"Realise that the Self is the self-contained mirror projecting and manifesting this world. The Self is pure unblemished consciousness. Be quick! Realise it quickly and gain transcendental happiness."[7]

Thus the "world as dream" or rather, in the above case, the "dream as world" is not only a favourite theme with sages but also with philosophers — both Eastern and Western, both ancient and modern.

---

7. Swami Sri Ramanananda Saraswathi, tr., *Tripurā Rahasya or the Mystery Beyond the Trinity,* Tiruvannamalai: Sri Ramanasramam, 1980, pp. 94-101.

2

The Antiquity of the Dream Metaphor in India

SOME of the earliest suggestions that the world may be like a dream have been traced by some scholars to the *Bṛhadāraṇyaka Upaniṣad* (circa 800 BC). The relevant passages run as follows (IV.3.18-20):

> As a great fish goes along both banks of a river, both the hither and the further, just so this person goes along both these conditions, the condition of sleeping and the condition of waking.
>
> As a falcon, or an eagle, having flown around here in space, becomes weary, folds its wings, and is borne down to its nest, just so this person hastens to that state where, asleep, he desires no desires and sees no dream.
>
> Verily, a person has those channels called *hita*; as a hair subdivided a thousandfold, so minute are they, full of white, blue, yellow, green, and red. Now when people seem to be killing him, when they seem to be overpowering him, when he seems to be falling into a hole — in these circumstances he is imagining through ignorance the very fear which he sees when awake. When, imagining that he is a god, that he is a king, he thinks "I am this world-all," that is his highest world.[1]

---

1. Robert Ernest Hume, tr., *The Thirteen Principal Upaniṣads*, Second edition, revised, London: Oxford University Press, 1968, p. 136.

R.E. Hume comments on IV.3.18 and IV.3.20 thus:

> "Verily, there are just two conditions of this person: the condition of being in this world and the condition of being in the other world. There is an intermediate third condition, namely, that of being in sleep" (*Brih*.4.3.9). Going to it, as a fish goes over to the other side of a river and back, one may have an actual experience of that reality of bliss in contrast *with which the waking life is but a bad dream* (*Brih*.4.3.18).[2]
>
> *Brih*.4.3.20 meets the same difficulty — that in a person's dreaming sleep people seem to be killing him, they seem to be overpowering him, an elephant seems to be tearing him to pieces, he seems to be falling into a hole — with the explanation that "he is imagining through ignorance the very fear which he sees when awake" and *which by implication is illusory*.[3]

Thus, Hume seems to suggest that waking life is compared in these passages to a bad dream, a comparison which carries with it the connotation of illusoriness.

This conclusion is difficult to defend from a reading of the text. Hume seems to anachronistically read later philosophical ideas into the text, a direction not taken by S. Radhakrishnan.[4] Even when the concept of *māyā* is introduced in the *Śvetāśvatara Upaniṣad* (IV.10) it is *not* connected with the dream-state, nor when it is mentioned earlier in the *Ṛgveda* (X.177).

A clearer indication of the "world as dream" idea is found in the famous text, the *Māṇḍūkyakārikā* of Gauḍapāda (circa. seventh century). Gauḍapāda "at times blurs the distinction between waking and dream consciousness, a distinction which

2. *Ibid.*, p. 45, emphasis added.
3. *Ibid.*, note 1, emphasis added.
4. S. Radhakrishnan, ed., *The Principal Upaniṣads*, London: George Allen & Unwin, 1953, pp. 251-62.

Śaṅkara later insists upon, and suggests that the whole of our waking experience is exactly the same as an illusory and insubstantial dream."[5]

Gauḍapāda's espousal of the view, that the world may be a dream, is unabashed and needs to be cited for that very reason. We must also thereafter take into account the possibility that the view originated in Buddhist circles and was later appropriated by Hindu thinkers.

KĀRIKĀS ON THE MĀṆḌŪKYA UPANIṢAD

The wise declare the insubstantiality of all things (seen) in a dream because they are within (the body) and are therein confined.

As in a dream state so in the waking state, the objects seen are insubstantial because of their being perceived. The difference between them is only that the objects of dream are confined within the body.

If in both states the objects are unreal, who is it that perceived these objects? Who is it that imagines them?

The self-luminous Self (*Ātman*) imagines Itself through Itself by the power of Its own illusion. It is Itself the cognizer of objects. This is the definite conclusion of the Vedānta.

The Lord (Self) imagines in various forms the well-defined objects which are in His mind when His mind is turned outward, and (various ideas) when His mind is turned within.

As a rope which is not clearly perceived is, in the dark, imagined to be a snake or a line of water, so the Self is imagined in different ways.

As definite knowledge of the rope destroys all illusions about

5. Eliot Deutsch and J.A.B. van Buitenen, *A Source Book of Advaita Vedānta*, Honolulu: The University Press of Hawaii, 1971, p. 119.

> it and the conviction arises that it is nothing but a rope, so is the nature of the Self determined.
>
> As a dream and illusion or a castle in the air are seen (to be unreal), so this whole universe is seen by those who are wise in Vedānta.[6]

It has been claimed that Gauḍapāda aligns himself with śūnyavāda and vijñānavāda of the Buddhists, that "In fact, he represents the best in Nāgārjuna and Vasubandhu,"[7] though the exact construction to be put on the convergence between Gauḍapāda and Mahāyanā Buddhism remains a matter of contention.[8] But as the theme of the world as dream clearly appears in the writing of Asaṅga and Vasubandhu (circa fourth century CE),[9] the emergence of this theme in recognizable form is determinately Buddhist. In fact, a fascinating application of the idea is already met within the *Aṣṭasāhasrikā Prajñapāramitā*, assignable to the second century BC as it was translated into Chinese in 172 AD by Lomaharṣa.[10]

> Thereupon the thought came to some of the gods in that assembly: What the fairies talk and murmur, that we understand though mumbled. What Subhūti has just told us, that we do not understand!
>
> Subhūti read their thoughts and said: There is nothing to understand, there is nothing to understand. For nothing in particular has been indicated, nothing in particular has been explained.

---

6. *Ibid.*, p. 120.
7. Chandradhar Sharma, *A Critical Survey of Indian Philosophy*, London: Rider & Company, 1960, p. 251.
8. T.M.P. Mahadevan, *Gauḍapāda: A Study in Early Advaita*, University of Madras (Chennai), 1960, Chapter IX.
9. G.P. Malalasekera, ed., *Encyclopedia of Buddhism*, Government of Ceylon (Sri Lanka), 1966, vol. II, p. 136 note 14.
10. *Ibid.*, p. 252.

Thereupon the gods thought: May the holy Subhūti enlarge on this! May the holy Subhūti enlarge on this! What the holy Subhūti here explores, demonstrates and teaches, that is remoter than the remote, subtler than the subtle, deeper than the deep.

Subhūti read their thoughts, and said: No one can attain any of the fruits of the holy life, or keep it:

- from the Stream-winner's fruit to full enlightenment unless he patiently accepts this elusiveness of the Dharma.

Then those gods thought: What should one wish those to be like who are worthy to listen to the doctrine from the holy Subhūti?

Subhūti read their thoughts, and said: Those who learn the doctrine from me one should wish to be like an illusory magical creation, for they will neither hear my words, nor experience the facts which they express.

The gods: Beings that are like a magical illusion, are they not just an illusion?

Subhūti: Like a magical illusion are those beings, like a dream. For magical illusion and beings are not two different things, nor are dreams and being. All objective facts (Dharmas) also are like a magical illusion, like a dream. The various classes of Saints — from Stream-winner to Buddhahood — also are like a magical illusion, like a dream.

The gods: A fully enlightened Buddha also, you say, is like a magical illusion, is like a dream? Buddhahood also, you say, is like a magical illusion, is like a dream?

Subhūti: Even Nirvāṇa, I say, is like a magical illusion, is like a dream. How much more so anything else!

The gods: Even Nirvāṇa, holy Subhūti, you say is like an illusion, is like a dream?

Subhūti: Even if perchance there could be anything more distinguished, of that too I would say that it is like an illusion, like a dream. For illusion and Nirvāṇa are not two different things, nor are dreams and Nirvāṇa.

Thereupon the Venerable Śāriputra, the Venerable Pūrṇa, son of Maitrāyaṇī, the Venerable Mahākaśyapa, and the other great Disciples, together with many thousands of Bodhisattvas, said: Who Subhūti, will be those who grasp this perfection of wisdom as here explained?

Thereupon the Venerable Ānanda said to those Elders: Bodhisattvas who cannot fall back will grasp it, or persons who have reached sound views, or Arhats in whom the outflows have dried up.

Subhūti: No one will grasp this perfection of wisdom as here explained, (i.e. explained in such a way that there is really no explanation at all). For no *dharma* at all has been indicated, lit up, or communicated. So there will be no one who can grasp it.[11]

A more romantic adaptation of the "world as a dream" is found in the *Śikṣāsamuccaya* of Śāntideva (seventh century).

"The senses are as though illusions and their objects as dreams. For instance, a sleeping man might dream that he had made love to a beautiful country girl, and he might remember her when he awoke. What do you think — does the beautiful girl he dreamed of really exist?"

"No, Lord."

"And would the man be wise to remember the girl of his dreams, or to believe that he had really made love to her?"

"No, Lord, because she doesn't exist at all, so how could he have made love to her — though of course he might think he did under the influence of weakness or fatigue."

"In just the same way a foolish and ignorant man of the

11. *Aṣṭasāhasrikā* II. 38-40. See Edward Conze, *et al.*, eds., *Buddhist Texts Through the Ages*, New York: Philosophical Library, 1954, pp. 177-78.

> world sees pleasant forms and believes in their existence. Hence he is pleased, and so he feels passion and acts accordingly . . . But from the very beginning, his actions are feeble, impeded, wasted, and changed in their course by circumstances . . . And when he ends his days, as the time of death approaches, his vitality is obstructed with the exhaustion of his allotted span of years, the karma that fell to his lot dwindles, and hence his previous actions form the object of the last thought of his mind as it disappears. Then, just as the man on first waking from sleep thinks of the country girl about whom he dreamed, the first thought on rebirth arises from two causes — the last thought of the previous life as its governing principle, and the actions of the previous life as its basis. Thus a man is reborn in the purgatories, or as an animal, a spirit, a demon, a human being, or a god . . . The stopping of the last thought is known as decease, the appearance of the first thought as rebirth. Nothing passes from life to life, but decease and rebirth take place nevertheless . . . But the last thought, the actions (karma), and the first thought, when they arise come from nowhere and when they cease go nowhere, for all are essentially defective, or themselves empty . . . In the whole process no one acts and no one experiences the results of action, except by verbal convention.[12]

The idea of the "world as dream," then, it would appear, became firmly lodged in Indian thought, and perhaps in the Indian psyche as well, by the seventh century after assuming definite shape after the first few centuries of the Christian era. The core content of the idea may be said to consist of the formulation that "the world is like a dream. A dream is merely an awareness of ideas; the corresponding objects are not really there. Just as one perceives the lack of objectivity in the dream

---

12. Wm. Theodore de Bary *et al.*, *Sources of Indian Tradition*, Delhi: Motilal Banarsidass, 1963, pp. 178-79.

pictures after one has woken up, so the lack of objectivity in the perceptions of waking life is perceived by those who have been awakened by the knowledge of true reality."[13]

One would expect the idea of the "world as dream" to appear in Śaṅkara's writings, even though he is more cautious than Gauḍapāda in equating the waking state with the dream. It does not come as a surprise then that one of the popular manuals of Advaita ascribed to him, the *Vivekacūdāmaṇi* contains many allusions to the "world as dream."

It is an Advaitic doctrine that though we apparently seem to possess one physical "body," we, in fact, possess more than one body and that one of them is a "dream body," in which we undergo dream experiences. Formal Advaita acknowledges three such bodies — the gross (*sthūla*), the subtle (*sūkṣma*) and the causal (*kāraṇa*). In the following verse, the fleeting nature of the association with the dream-body, and epiphenomemal bodies emanating from the physical body, is urged as a consideration for dissolving the self-evident identity with the physical body itself.

> Just as thou dost not identify thyself with the shadow-body (1), the image-body (2), the dream-body (3), or the body thou has in the imaginations of thy heart, cease thou to do likewise with the living body (4) also.[14]

---

13. Edward Conze, *Buddhism: Its Essence and Development*, New York: Harper & Row, 1959, p. 168.

14. Swami Madhavananda, tr., *Vivekacūdāmaṇi of Śrī Śaṅkarācārya*, Calcutta (Kolkata): Advaita Āshram, 1966, p. 64.

    [(1) Shadow-body — The shadow of thy body.

    (2) Image-body — The image or reflection of thy body, case in water, etc.

    (3) Dream-body — The body that thou mayest assume in dreams.

    (4) Living-body — The gross body, with the prāṇas, etc.]

The other verses pertain more directly to the idea of the "world as dream."

Verse 170:

> In dreams, when there is no actual contact with the external world, the mind alone creates the whole universe consisting of the experiencer*, etc.[15] Similarly, in the waking state also, there is no difference. Therefore, all this (phenomenal universe) is the projection of the mind.

Verse 199:

> *Avidyā* or Nescience and its effects are likewise considered as beginningless. But with the rise of *vidyā* or realization, the entire effects of *avidyā*, even though beginningless, are destroyed together with their root** — like dreams on waking up from sleep. It is clear that the phenomenal universe, even though without beginning, is not eternal — like previous non-existence.[16***]

Verse 234:

> If the universe be true, let it then be perceived in the state of deep sleep also. As it is not at all perceived, it must be unreal and false, like dreams.[17]

---

* The experiencer, etc. — That is, the experiencer, the experienced, and experience: subject, object, and their coming into relation.]

15. *Ibid.*, p. 67.

16. *Ibid.*, p. 79.

17. *Ibid.*, p. 93.

** Root — Avidyā:

*** Previous non-existence — Pragabhava, a term of Hindu logic. When we say a thing comes into being at a definite point of time, we imply also that there was non-existence of that particular thing prior to that moment. And this "non-existence" is obviously beginningless. But, it ceases as soon as the thing comes into being. Similarly, *avidyā*, even though beginningless, disappears when realization comes.

Verses 252, 253:

As the place, time, objects, knower, etc. called up in dreams are all unreal, so is also the world experienced here in the waking state, for it is all an effect of one's own ignorance. Because this body, the organs, the prāṇas, egoism, etc. are also thus unreal, therefore are thou that serene, pure, Supreme *Brahman*, the One without a second.

(What is) erroneously supposed to exist in something, is when the truth about it has been known, nothing but that substratum, and not at all different from it: The diversified, dream universe (appears and) passes away in the dream itself. Does it appear on waking as something distinct from one's own Self?[18]

Verse 425:

Freed from all sense of reality of the external sense-objects on account of his always remaining merged in *Brahman*; only seeming[*] to enjoy such sense-objects as are offered by others, like one sleepy, or like a child; beholding this world as one seen in dreams, and having cognition of it as chance moments — rare indeed is such a man, the enjoyer[19**] of the fruits of endless merit, and he alone is blessed and esteemed on earth.

Verses 447, 448:

Through the realization of one's identity with *Brahman*, all the accumulated actions of a hundred crore of cycles come to naught, like the actions of the dream-state on awakening.

---

18. *Ibid.*, pp. 101-02.

* Only seeming etc. — When his attendants or friends offer him food, etc. he takes it but half consciously, his mind being deeply absorbed in *Brahman*.

19. *Ibid.*, pp. 166-67.

** The enjoyer, etc. — That is, a most fortunate man.

> Can the good actions or dreadful sins that a man fancies himself doing in the dream-state, lead him to heaven or hell after he has awakened from sleep?[20]

Verse 454:

> For the sage who lives in his own Self as *Brahman*, the One without a second, devoid of identification with the limiting adjuncts, the question of the existence of prarabhda work is meaningless, like the question of a man who has awakened from sleep having any connection with the objects seen in the dream-state.[21]

Verse 457:

> Similarly, he who is absorbed in *Brahman* lives identified with that eternal reality and beholds nothing else. As one has a memory of the objects seen in a dream, so the man of realization has a memory of the everyday actions such as eating.[22]

Verse 516:

> O Master, thou hast out of sheer grace awakened me from sleep and completely saved me, who was wandering in an interminable dream, in a forest of birth, decay, and death created by illusion, being tormented day after day by countless afflictions, and sorely troubled by the tiger of egoism.[23]

The changes run on the dream metaphor during the course of this text are truly amazing in their variety. The medium is not just the message here: several messages are being delivered through the same medium of the dream metaphor. The process

---

20. *Ibid.*, pp. 173-74.
21. *Ibid.*, p. 176.
22. *Ibid.*, p. 177.
23. *Ibid.*, p. 199.

of *saṁsāra* itself is compared to a dream; the process of *involvement* in it is likened to a dream; the process of *stepping* out of it is compared to stepping out of a dream and the state of the world in the *post-realization* phase is compared to a dream and of course the world as such as *pre-realization* phase is referred to a dream. It is all, well, a dream!

Interesting features distinguish the use of the dream-metaphor within Hinduism and Buddhism. While the nuances of the metaphor as such are more clearly captured within Hinduism, wherein it is treated as a multi-faceted gem to be looked at from many angles, a clearer attempt is made in Buddhism to distinguish the texture of this metaphor from such others as may be used in a similar context. Evidence in support of the point made regarding the nature of the deployment of the dream metaphor in Hinduism will be presented in the pages that follow. At this point, the claim regarding the more graded use of the dream metaphor in Buddhism than say, as employed by Śaṅkara above, needs to be substantiated. Śaṅkara's use is skilful and versatile, and makes a general point effectively. It is not that dream metaphor has also not been employed generally as illustrating the irreality of the world within Buddhism as well. It is indeed so used in the *Laṅkāvatāra-Sūtra*, which was translated into Chinese for the first time in 430 AD.

> It is as if some man, asleep, dreams of a country, full of women and men, elephants, horses, cars, pedestrians, villages, cities and market towns, cows, buffaloes, woods, parks, and adorned with various mountains, rivers and lakes. In his dream, he enters the woman's apartments of the king's palace, and then he wakes up. Awake, his memory runs back over the country and the woman's apartments. It would not be an intelligent thing to do for this man, to go in his memory through the various unreal experiences which

> he had in his dream, or would it, Mahāmati? In the same way, the foolish common people, bitten by false views and under the influence of the heretics, do not realise that what is seen by their own mind is like a dream, and they rely on notions of oneness and otherness, of being and non-being.[24]

What one has in mind at the moment, however, are the fine distinctions found in the *Mahāyānasaṅgraha* of Asaṅga, with some comments of Vasubandhu. In this series, each metaphor is adapted to a certain question in a catechismal progression of charming sophistication, so appealing in fact that it deserves to be cited in toto.

1. One may ask, "How can the non-existent become a sense-object?" In order to remove this doubt, the Sūtra compares things to a magical illusion.
2. One may ask, "How can thought and mental acts arise without an object?" To remove this doubt, there is the comparison to a mirage. Here thought and mental acts correspond to the mirage, and the object to the water. When a mirage makes its appearance, no real water is there, and yet the notion of real water arises.
3. One may ask, "How, in the absence of an object, can one experience desirable and undesirable impressions." To remove this doubt, things are compared to a dream. In a dream also there is no real object, and yet pleasant and unpleasant impressions are felt.
4. One may ask, "How, in the absence of an object, can wholesome and unwholesome actions produce desirable or undesirable fruits?" In answer, things are compared to an image. The image is not the real object. It is relative to a model that one produces the notion

24. Edward Conze, ed., *op. cit.*, p. 213.

of an image. Yet, as distinct from the model, it has no reality. Likewise, a desirable or undesirable fruit, though unreal, can be perceived.

5. One may ask, "How, in the absence of objects, can different acts of consciousness arise?" In answer, things are compared to a reflection. In a shadow play, one sees all sorts of things reflected. Although these reflections are seen, they are not really what they seem to be. In the same way, acts of consciousness are not different things, although they appear to be so.
6. One may ask, "How, in the absence of objects, can different verbal expressions arise?" In answer, things are compared to an echo. An echo is not a real sound, and yet it is heard. Similarly, verbal expressions are not real things, and yet they are understood.
7. One may ask, "How, in the absence of an object, can the images apperceived in trance arise?" In answer, things are compared to the moon reflected in water. The moon reflected in water is not really in the water, and yet, because the water is wet and limpid, the moon is seen in it. So, with concentrated thought, the objects which form its range are not real things, and yet, they are perceived, the state of trance playing the part of the water.
8. One may ask, "How, in the absence of an object, can Bodhisattvas, whose thought is unperverted, be born at will for the service of beings?" In answer, things are compared to a magical creation. A magical creation is not a real thing, and yet a conjurer has the power to conjure up all sorts of objects, which can be perceived. The same holds good here. The personality which a

> Bodhisattva assumes is not real, and yet it is perceived when he works for the benefit of beings.[25]

This sophistication is displayed both vertically and horizontally. In the following commentary by Vasubandhu on the verse cited at the outset, nine different perspectives on *saṁsāric* existence are presented through nine different metaphors used for it, including that of the dream.

> As stars, a fault of vision, as a lamp,
> A mock show, dew drops, or a bubble,
> A dream, a lightning flash, or cloud,
> So we should view what is conditioned.
>
> Commentary: The marks of the *elements of saṁsāric existence should be considered from nine points of view:*
>
> 1. As regards their *visibility,* all mental constituents disappear when right gnosis is realised, just as stars disappear when the sun shines.
> 2. As regards the *sign,* because things are wrongly perceived, just as the hairs in front of the eyes of a man who has an eye disease.
> 3. As regards *consciousness,* which is like a lamp, because passions are born insofar as things are seen.
> 4. As regards their *support,* the elements composing this world are essentially unreal like things appearing in a mock show.
> 5. As regards the *body,* which lasts for a short time, like drops of dew.
> 6. As regards *fruition,* which is like a bubble.
> 7. As regards the *past,* because like dreams the things of the past remain only as a memory.

---

25. *Ibid.*, pp. 215-16.

8. As regards the *present*, because this disappears quickly like lightning.
9. As regards the *future*, which is like clouds, because the store consciousness contains all the seeds of the elements which are going to develop.

Vajracchedikā 32a, Asaṅga Saptati, v. 76, and Vasubandhu's Commentary.[26]

26. *Ibid.*, p. 161.

3

The Dream-Metaphor in Western Religion and Thought

THIS preliminary survey of the dream metaphor in the Indic religious tradition may be supplemented with a survey of the evidence of its presence in the Abrahamic religious tradition.

Dreams have played an interesting role in the religious history in the geographical region where the ancient religions of the world, including Judaism, emerged:

> The fantastic, yet vivid nature of dream-imagery inevitably impresses the unsophisticated mind with conviction of having made contact with another order of existence. Ancient Egyptian literature provides much evidence of such reaction: a notable instance is Thothmes IV's dream, under shadow of the Sphinx, of appearance of the sun-god who requested him to free his image (the Sphinx) for encroaching sand. Keys for interpretation of dreams as foretelling the future were produced in Egypt. Similarly, Mesopotamian literature attests religious importance of dreams. The Sumerian word Ma-Mu meant "creation of the night," and was closely related to sleep and death. In Epic Gilgamesh, Enkidu dreams of his coming death; Gudea of Lagash practised incubation to learn the will of god Ningirsu concerning building of a temple. Elaborate keys to dream-interpretations were also compiled. Belief in dreams as warning of the future abound in the Bible (e.g., Joseph's dream and his ability as dream-interpreter (Gen. 40:5ff.);

Paul's dreams (Acts 23:11; 27:23)). Greek literature provides abundant testimony to belief that dreams had divine origins and were prophetic: the custom of incubation was well established. Dreams figure much in medieval Christian literature, and could have either divine or demonic origins; dreams of sexual nature were attributed to latter source.[1]

The idea however that, apart from dreams being part of existence in the world, they could also provide a paradigm for the nature of the existence of the world itself as such does not seem to have emerged.

One can identify a twofold division of dreams in early Judaism. One type would be a "message dream" (a communication from God to a King or a Prophet in which the dreamer is no more than a medium) such as in Genesis 41:1 ff, or a dream which is a more direct expression of divinity, (e.g. Numbers 12:6) and the other would be an apocalyptic dream such as described in Ezekeil (1:4-28).[2]

In Egypt, in Mesopotamia, in Israel and later in Christianity as well, the medium of the dream never became the message of the nature of the world — only a means of delivering a message in the world. The prophetic element was primary even in Greece and Rome, and dreams, like oracles, were chiefly a means of divination. "Though theories of divination are linked with science and religion, encompassing both knowledge and belief, they cannot in our context be used in any way to dichotomize the two. Those who suppose that knowledge is unitary, or, at the very least, that ignorance is

1. S.G.F. Brandon, ed., *A Dictionary of Comparative Religion,* New York: Macmillan Publishing Company, 1970, pp. 247-48.
2. Benjamin Kilborne, "Dreams" in Mircea Eliade, editor-in-chief, *The Encyclopaedia of Religion,* New York: Macmillan Publishing Company, 1987, Volume 4, p. 482.

monolithic, cannot understand how beliefs in dreams and oracles could express a theory of knowledge."[3]

Greek thought offers an occasional suggestion of the dreamlike quality of a part of the world, or of the existence in it, or of the world itself. In fact, dreams have played a significant but limited role in the history of Greek culture. The prophetic and oracular role of dreams was recognized early on in Greek culture,[4] but they do not seem to play the same role in Greek thought. If dream was used as a metaphor at all, it was a metaphor not for the world, but for the *underworld*. People led the same kind of shadowy existence in the Hades, as figures do in dreams.[5]

If anything, it was sleep or rather darkness associated with sleep which is a much more potent motif, as in Plato's allegory of the cave. All these ideas seem to find their proper place in the following introduction to that allegory by F.M. Cornford:

The Allegory of the Cave

> The progress of the mind from the lowest state of unenlightenment to knowledge of the Good is now illustrated by the famous parable comparing the world of appearance to an underground Cave. In Empedocles' religious poem, the powers which conduct the soul to his incarnation say, "We have come under this cavern's roof." The image was probably taken from mysteries held in caves or dark chambers representing the underworld, through which the candidates for initiation were led to the revelation of sacred objects in a blaze of light. The idea that the body is

---

3. *Ibid.*, p. 483.
4. Francis Macdonald Cornford, *Plato's Cosmology*, London: Routledge & Kegan Paul Ltd., 1956, p. 288.
5. See J. Bruce Long, "Underworld," in Mircea Eliade, Editor in Chief, *op. cit.*, vol. 15, pp. 134-35.

> a prison-house, to which the soul is condemned for past misdeeds, is attributed by Plato to the Orphics.
>
> One moral of the allegory is drawn from the distress caused by a too sudden passage from darkness to light. The earlier warning against plunging untrained minds into the discussion of moral problems, as the Sophists and Socrates himself had done, is reinforced by the picture of the dazed prisoner dragged out into the sunlight. Plato's ten years' course of pure mathematics is to habituate the intellect to abstract reasoning before moral ideas are called in question.[6]

It is interesting to speculate on what the introduction of "dream" as intermediate stage between the "passage from darkness to light" might have implied for the allegory. For to allegorize the allegory further, darkness would then correspond to the "sleep" of ignorance, and light, of course, light to knowledge. Advaitic thought makes a lot of the intervening liminal phase between utter darkness and complete light, unlike the Greek. The following passage sheds some light on how the universe might be an epiphany of semi-darkness. It contains a few opaque terms which are technical to Advaita but the point it makes seems clear enough:

> The light must be dim in order to enable the ego to rise up. In broad daylight a rope does not look like a snake. The rope itself cannot be seen in thick darkness; so there is no chance of mistaking it for a snake. Only in dim light, in the dusk, in light darkened by shadows or in darkness lighted by a dim light does the mistake occur of a rope seeming a snake. Similarly, it is for the Pure Radiant Being to rise up as the Ego — it is possible only in Its Light diffused through darkness. This darkness is otherwise known as the Original

---

6. Francis Macdonald Cornford, tr., *The Republic of Plato*, Oxford: Clarendon Press, 1955, p. 222.

> Ignorance (Original Sin). The Light passing through it is called Reflected Light. *The Reflected Light on its own merits is commonly known as the Pure mind or Īśvara or God.* Īśvara is well-known to be unified with *Māyā*; in other words, the Reflected Light is Īśvara.[7]

There is a direct reference in Plato to individual dreams but it is somewhat negative in tone; one might say it takes a dim view of dreams as potentially metaphysical metaphor. It is more in line with Freud, although Freud might demur, where it seems somewhat connected with the idea of wish-fulfilment.

> *What Kind of Desires do you Mean?*
>
> Those which bestir themselves in dreams, when the gentler part of the soul slumbers and the control of reason is withdrawn; then the wild beast in us, full-fed with meat or drink, becomes rampant and shakes off sleep to go in quest of what will gratify its own instincts. As you know, it will cast away all shame and prudence at such moments and stick at nothing. In fantasy, it will not shrink from intercourse with a mother or anyone else, man, god, or brute, or from forbidden food or any deed of blood. In a word, it will go to any length of shamelessness and folly.[8]

The context of the discussion however is political. As Cornford explains:

> In the individual soul, despotism means the dominion of one among those unlawful appetites whose existence, even in decent people, is revealed in dreams. The democratic man allowed equal rights to all his desires; but his balance is easily destroyed by the growth of a master passion, which

---

7. *Talks with Sri Ramana Maharshi*, Tiruvannamalai: Sri Ramanasramam, 1984, pp. 286-87.
8. Francis Macdonald Cornford, tr., *op. cit.*, p. 290.

> will gradually enslave every other element in the soul. So, at last, the portrait of the perfectly unjust man is completed for comparison with the perfectly just philosopher-king.[9]

It would perhaps not be superfluous to add that for Aristotle (384-322 BC) "dreams are natural, not supernatural. Thus he denies that dreams ever come from outside the dreamer's physical sensations and memories,"[10] a line of thought curiously enough used in Hindu thought to generate the possibility that the world we live in could be of our own making, like a dream.

It is clear, therefore, that while in the pre-modern West dream had a metaphorical role to play in a philosophical context, it substituted for the expression of base instincts. It continued to play an occult role, as in dreams of prophecy, and a mystical role in the lives of the saints but from an Eastern standpoint, one feels shortchanged in Western thought until one comes to Descartes via the following route:

> Generally speaking, Christianity eliminated external magical rites of divination and substituted prayer, thus leaving room for dreams, visions, and prophetic inspirations, provided these were God-sent. Even in Christianity, however, the possibility of doubt remained; was the dream sent by God or not? Indeed, Luther prayed to God not to send him any dreams whatever, so he would not have to deal with the question.
>
> The matter of deceitful dreams is very old indeed. In the Odyssey, there are true and false dreams that not even the gods can tell apart with any certainty. For Homer, deception is a fact of existence; gods deceive mortals as they deceive one another. Zeus, for example, sends Agamemnon a divine dream that incites him to fight the Greeks in a battle he is

9. *Ibid.*, p. 281.

10. Benjamin Kilbourne, *op. cit.*, p. 484.

> destined to lose. It is Penelope who explains that dreams escape by two doors, one of horn, the other of ivory (Odyssey 19.560 ff.). Dreams passing through the gate of ivory are deceptive and vain; those by the gate of horn, veridical. All this is well and good, but the question remains: how does one not tell what sort of dream one has had? These difficulties increased when God was given the attributes of omniscience and omnipotence, for this meant that by definition God could not deceive. Indeed, these questions did not go away; in his Discourse on Method (1637) Descartes wrestled valiantly with the implications of the issue of dreams and doubt and the existence of God.[11]

There are some passages in Plato suggestive of the dreamlike quality of the world. In Hindu thought, when the world is compared to a dream in the context of treating it as *māyā*, the discussion sometimes begins with the recognition of its changeability and often slides in the direction of the changeability of the larger universe, which is treated as an indication of its unreality and hence a confirmation of its nature as *māyā*.[12] There are hints of such changeability involving an element of unreality in Plato:[13]

> Notwithstanding these hints, however, one cannot overlook the fact that Plato's philosophy is an idealism of the ideals, and not of ideas in the sense of mental states. He uses the term ideas also, and tells us that they only, as contrasted with physical things, are real. But his ideas are patterns or

---

11. *Ibid.*, p. 484.
12. M. Hiriyanna, *The Essentials of Indial Philosophy*, London: George Allen & Unwin, 1948, p. 160: David Goodman, ed., *The Teachings of Sri Ramana Maharshi*, New York: Arkana, 1985, pp. 190-91.
13. For an interesting discussion see I.M. Crombie, *An Examination of Plato's Doctrines*, New York: Routledge & Kegan Paul, 1962, Volume I, p. 42ff.

> standards for the things of sense. The idea of man is the ideal man, and the idea of horse is the ideal horse. They are also called concepts or forms. Reality, for Plato, is a system of these ideals, all interconnected by the supreme ideal of the good. Plato did not conceive of subjectivism or mentalism, though the germs of the theory were not wanting in the philosophy of the sophists who preceded him.[14]

Descartes (1596-1650) provides an example of a major Western philosopher who tried to come to grips with the idea of the world as dream, not directly to be sure, but in his conceptual struggle to establish the distinction between waking and dreaming. As the issue has not been raised to the same level of plausibility in early Western thought as in Indian — except for some clues in Plato as already indicated — an examination of Descartes' views in detail will not be out of place. It will also probably not be out of place to cite Descartes' reflections in extenso in view of the relative paucity of discussion in Western thought on this issue.

Descartes allows for the possibility that distinguishing between dreaming and waking may not be a simple matter, on grounds with which we are already somewhat familiar. However, he finally accepts the primacy of waking state over the dreaming state on the ground that (1) the criterion of reality, when brought in relation to God, would ensure that we are not deceived in waking; (2) the criterion of reality, when brought in relation to reason over imagination, suggests the same even if reason is not infallible. Thus both on grounds of revelation and reason, so to say, the waking state is the real one. The passage in which these points are made by him runs as follows:

---

14. P.T. Raju, *Idealistic Thought of India*, London: George Allen & Unwin, 1953, p. 44.

Finally, if there are still men who are not sufficiently persuaded of the existence of God and of their soul by the reasons I have given, I would like them to know that all the other things of which they think themselves perhaps more assured, such as having a body, and that there are stars and an earth, and such like, are less certain; for, although we may have a *moral assurance* of these things, which is such that it seems that, short of being foolish, no one can doubt their existence, at the same time also, short of being unreasonable, when it is a question of a *metaphysical certainty*, one cannot deny that there are not sufficient grounds for being absolutely assured, when one observes that one can in the same way imagine, being asleep, that one has another body, and that one sees other stars and another earth, without there being anything of the sort. For how does one know that the thoughts which come while one dreams are false rather than the others, seeing that they are often no less strong and clear? And may the most intelligent men study this question as much as they please, I do not believe that they can give any reason which would be sufficient to remove this doubt, unless they presuppose the existence of God. For, firstly, even the rule which I stated above that I held, namely, that the things we grasp very clearly and very distinctly are all true, is assured only because God is or exists, and because he is a perfect Being, and because everything that is in us comes from him; whence it follows that our ideas and notions, being real things and coming from God, in so far as they are clear and distinct, cannot to this extent be other than true. Accordingly, if we often enough have ideas which contain errors, they can only be those which contain something confused and obscure, because in this they participate in nothingness, that is to say that they are in us in this confused way only because we are not completely perfect. And it is evident that it is no less contradictory that error or imperfection, as such, should proceed from God, than that truth or perfection should come from nothingness. But, if we did not know that all that is in us which is real and true comes from a perfect and infinite Being, we would have no reason which would assure us that, however clear and distinct our ideas might be, they had the perfection of being true.

But, after knowledge of God and of the soul has thus made us certain of this rule, it is a simple matter to understand that the dreams we imagine when we are asleep should not in any way make us doubt the truth of the thoughts we have when we are awake. For, even if it should happen that, while sleeping, one should have some quite distinct idea, as, for example, if a geometer were to discover some new demonstration, his being asleep would not prevent it from being true; and as for the most ordinary error of our dreams, which consists in representing to us various objects in the same way as our waking senses do, it does not matter that they give us occasion to doubt the truth of such ideas, because they can also lead us into error often enough without our being asleep, as when those who have jaundice see everything yellow, or when the stars or other very distant bodies seem to us smaller than they are. For, finally, whether we are awake or asleep, we should never let ourselves be persuaded except on the evidence of our reason. And, it is to be observed that I say: of our reason, and not of our imagination or our senses. For, although we see the sun very clearly, we should not on that account judge that it is only as large as we see it; and we can well imagine distinctly a lion's head grafted onto the body of a goat, without concluding on that account that there is any such chimera in the world; for reason does not dictate that what we see or imagine thus is true, but it does tell us that all our ideas and notions must have some basis in truth, for it would not be possible that God, who is all perfect and true, should have put them in us unless it were so. And because our reasoning

> is never so clear or complete while we sleep as when we are awake, even though sometimes our imaginations are as vivid and distinct or even more so, reason tells us that, it not being possible that our thoughts should all be true, because we are not absolutely perfect, what truth there is in them will undoubtedly be found in those we have when we are awake rather than those we have in our dreams.[15]

One of the arguments used by Descartes to question the equation of waking with dream state is the argument by falsity. This is best summarized by K.C. Bhattacharyya's statement that "dreams do not deny the truth of waking life as a whole . . . Waking, however, denies the truth of dreams."[16] Interestingly, this argument — what I have called *the argument by falsity* — is *not* utilized by Descartes to establish the epistemological superiority of waking over dreaming because he is not quite sure of the truth of the waking state per se, except by bringing it in relation to God. He does, however, accept the argument that the waking state is less likely to be false relative to dreaming. He also uses, independently of God, argument by memory, namely, that memory establishes a connectedness between waking states lacking in dreaming. This argument, however, differs from what I have elsewhere called the *argument by memory*, namely, that while we remember dream experiences in waking, we do not *remember* waking experiences in dreams, even though waking experience may often provide the *content* of dreams. And this argument too is not employed by Descartes. By relying on revelation and

15. Rene Descartes, *Discourse on Method and the Meditations*, Harmonsworth: Penguin Books, 1972: translated by P.E. Sutcliffe, pp. 48-50.

16. Quoted in William M. Indich, *Consciousness in Advaita Vedānta*, Delhi: Motilal Banarsidass, 1980, p. 63.

reason, he is able to overcome his earlier hesitation as to whether there were adequate grounds for distinguishing between waking and dreaming. Another relevant passage from the *Meditations* relevant to this point is cited below:

> Whence it is quite manifest that, notwithstanding the sovereign goodness of God, the nature of man, in so far as it is composed of mind and body, cannot sometimes be other than faulty and deceptive.
>
> For if there is any cause which arouses, not in the foot, but in one of the parts of the nerve which stretches from the foot up to the brain, or even into the brain itself, the same movement which ordinarily occurs when the foot is injured, pain will be felt as though it were in the foot, and the sense will naturally be deceived; for as the same movement in the brain can but cause the same feeling in the mind, and as this feeling is much more frequently aroused by a cause which hurts the foot than by one operating elsewhere, it is very much more reasonable that it should lead the mind to feel pain in the foot rather than in any other part. And although dryness of the throat does not always arise, as it usually does, from drink being necessary for the health of the body, but sometimes from quite an opposite reason, as is experienced by those with dropsy, yet it is much better that it should deceive in this case, than that, on the contrary, it should always deceive when the body is well, and the same holds true in other cases.
>
> And indeed this consideration is of the greatest service to me not only for recognizing all the errors to which my nature is subject, but also for avoiding them, or correcting them more easily: for, knowing that all my senses more usually indicate to me what is advantageous or disadvantageous to the body, and being almost always able to make use of several of these senses in the examination of the same object, and further, being able to make use of my memory to link

and join present knowledge to past, and of my understanding which has already discovered all the causes of my errors, *I must no longer fear henceforward that falsity may be met with in what is more commonly presented to me by my senses. And I must reject all the doubts of these last few days, as hyperbolical and ridiculous, particularly the general uncertainty about sleep, which I could not distinguish from the wakeful state: for now I see a very notable difference between the two states in that our memory can never connect our dreams with one another and with the general course of our lives, as it is in the habit of connecting the things which happen to us when we are awake.* And, in truth, if someone, when I am awake, appeared to me all of a sudden and as suddenly disappeared as do the images I see when I am asleep, so that I could see neither where he came from nor where he went, it would not be without reason that I deemed him to be a spectre or phantom formed in my brain, and similar to those which are formed there when I am asleep, rather than a real man. But when I perceive things of which I clearly know both the place they come from and that in which they are, and the time at which they appear to me, and when, without any interruption, I can link the perception I have of them with the whole of the rest of my life, I am fully assured that it is not in sleep that I am perceiving them but while I am awake. And I must not in any way doubt the truth of these things, if, after having called upon all my senses, my memory and my understanding to examine them, nothing is reported to me by anyone of these faculties which conflicts with what is reported to me by the others. For as God is not the deceiver, it follows necessarily that I am not deceived in this.

But because the necessities of action often oblige us to make a decision before we have had the leisure to examine things so carefully, it must be admitted that the life of man is very often subject to error in particular cases; and we must, in

> conclusion, recognize the infirmity and weakness of our nature.[17]

The third argument used to establish the primacy of waking state over dream is based on the *argument by materiality*: that the objects are experienced as external to us in the waking state despite the ambiguity which might sometimes attend them. Thus Descartes writes:

> But, God being no deceiver, it is manifest that he does not of himself send me these ideas directly, or by the agency of any creature in which their reality is not formally, but only eminently, contained. For, as he has not given me any faculty by which I can know that this is so, but on the contrary a very strong inclination to believe that they are sent to me or

---

17. Descatres, *op. cit.*, p. 167-68. The following observation of William Indich seems relevant here: "Thus, Śaṅkara argues that although the *dream content*, e.g., seeing oneself flying through space, is contradicted upon waking, the *dream experience* itself remains an empirically real fact, i.e., one has actually dreamed that one flew through space. Śaṅkara concludes two important points from this. First, he maintains that the content of dreams is as consistent in its own sphere as waking content is to the waking subject, since dream content is only sublated or contradicted upon waking. The fact that dream is incongruous with waking and waking is, likewise, incompatible with dream, establishes that the two spheres are *discontinuous from each other, and that each is equally autonomous in its own domain*. In this sense, Śaṅkara offers an implicit rejection of Descartes' attempt, in the Sixth Meditation, to distinguish waking from dreaming on the basis of the claim that the former is more consistent than the latter. *Second*, Śaṅkara maintains that dreaming perceptual experience is as real, in terms of phenomenal consciousness, as waking perceptual experience but that ultimately both are bound and illusory. And in this sense, Śaṅkara extends the discussion of philosophically relevant experience beyond the waking state and its conditions." (*Ibid.*, pp. 84-85).

> derive from corporeal things, I do not see how he could be excused of deception if in truth these ideas came from or were produced by causes other than corporeal things. And accordingly, one must confess that corporeal things exist.
>
> However, they are perhaps not exactly as we perceive them through the senses, for perception by the senses is very obscure and confused in many ways; but at least I must admit that *all that I conceive clearly and distinctly, that is to say, generally speaking, all that is comprised in the object of speculative geometry, is truly to be found in corporeal things*. But, as concerns other things, which are either only particular, as, for example, that the sun is of such a size and shape, etc., or are perceived less clearly and distinctly, as in the case of light, sound, pain, and so on, although they are very doubtful and uncertain, nevertheless, from the fact alone that God is not a deceiver, and that consequently he has permitted no falsity in my opinion, while he has not also given me some faculty capable of correcting, I believe I may conclude with assurance that I have within me the means of knowing these things with *certainty*.[18]

This argument too is different from what I have called the *argument by materiality or substantiality* — namely that objects of waking state are found to exist both before and after dreams but the objects of dreams vanish with them.

Two points can now be made with some measure of confidence. The first is that it would be misleading to cite Descartes as proof that "on careful analysis, . . . it is difficult to say which is real, the waking state or the dream state."[19] Sankaranarayanan seems to make such a claim when he goes

---

18. Descartes, *op. cit.*, p. 158.

19. P. Sankaranarayanan, *What Is Advaita?* Bombay (Mumbai): Bharatiya Vidya Bhavan, 1970, p. 46.

on to say: "In this connection, one is reminded of what Descartes says in his Meditations: 'When I consider the matter carefully, I do not find a single characteristic by means of which I can certainly determine whether I am awake or whether I am dreaming. The visions of a dream and the experience of my waking state are so much alike that I am completely puzzled and I do not really know if I am not dreaming at this moment.'"[20] It is true that this reflects a phase in Descartes' reflection but it does *not* reflect his conclusion.[21] Sankaranarayanan perhaps rests on safer ground when he cites Pascal as follows: "If a dream comes to us every night, we should be as much occupied with it as by the thing we see every day, and if an artisan were certain that he would dream every night for full twelve hours, that he was a King, then he would be just as happy as a King who dreams every night for twelve hours that he is an artisan."[22]

The second point is that there are Advaitic arguments to be urged against Descartes' position.[23] This is, however, not the place to investigate Descartes' arguments logically as this examination is to be attempted presently; rather the point to examine here is whether they can be countered metaphorically. We have six arguments in all — the argument by falsity (two versions), the argument by memory (two versions) and the argument by substantiality (two versions). All six can be met by double-barrelling the dream metaphor — by regarding the dream state as experienced by us as contained within a

20. *Ibid*.
21. Descartes, *op. cit.*, p. 168.
22. P. Sankaranarayanan, *op. cit.*, p. 47. The problem precisely is that what he *wishes* of the dream state *obtains* in the waking state.
23. Jadunath Sinha, *Indian Psychology: Cognition*, Calcutta (Kolkata): Sinha Publishing House, 1958, Volume I, p. 321.

longer dream state. This longer dream state, into which one would return from shorter dreams within it, will exhibit all the features which caused one to prefer waking to dreaming — without it being one!

One thus reverts to a central issue Descartes raised in the context of dream: that the distinction between waking and dreaming is by no means as self-evident as might seem to be the case. Both ordinary mortals but more so philosophers who have both preceded and succeeded him have at least raised the issue he mulls over:

> While we are having them, dreams often appear to be as real as waking experience; children have to be told that the object of their terror "was only a dream," hence not part of the world. William James expressed this well in his *Principles of Psychology*: "The world of dreams is our real world whilst we are sleeping, because our attention then lapses from the sensible world. Conversely, when we wake, the attention usually lapses from the dream-world and that becomes unreal." This similarity has led philosophers to pose the question, "How can you prove whether at this moment we are sleeping, and all our thoughts are a dream; or whether we are awake, and talking to one another in the waking state?" (Plato, *Theaetetus*, 158.) In perhaps the most famous example of the difficulty of distinguishing dreams from reality, Descartes introduced his method of universal doubt. He concluded, "I see so manifestly that there are no certain indications by which we may clearly distinguish wakefulness from sleep that I am lost in astonishment." (*First Meditation*.) Descartes finally resolved his doubts in this respect by appealing to a criterion of consistency: "For at present, I find a very notable difference between the two, inasmuch as our memory can never connect our dreams with one another, or with the whole course of our lives, as it

> unites events which happen to us while we are awake." (*Sixth Meditation.*)[24]

The consistency criterion adopted by Descartes and "by several more recent writers on the topic" is however considered seriously open to question by A.R. Manser on the following grounds: Firstly, "consistency can only be used as a test of a particular experience by waiting to see what happens in the future. It would enable me to tell that I had been dreaming, not that I am now dreaming; for however confident I am of the reality of my surroundings, something may happen in the future that will reveal them to be part of a dream."[25] Secondly, "in most cases, the dream convinces us that it is a reality, in that no doubt or questioning arises during its course. The difference between dreams and hallucinations lies in the fact that there is nothing external to dreams with which they can be compared, no tests that can be applied. For if we did apply a test in a dream, the result would be to confirm its reality. Philosophers have sought for some mark or test that would solve this problem, but there is none available. Any suggested sign of reality could be duplicated in the dream, and if all dreams bore marks of unreality, then there could not even be confusion over the remembering of them."[26]

These criticisms of the consistency criteria are remarkably reminiscent of the modern Advaitic formulations of the world

---

24. A.R. Manser, "Dreams" in Paul Edwards, Editor in Chief, *The Encyclopedia of Philosophy*, New York: The Macmillan Company and The Free Press, 1967, Volume Two, p. 417.
25. *Ibid.*, p. 417.
26. *Ibid.*

as dream[27] and one may now turn to a consideration of these formulations.[28]

Modern exponents of Advaita have used the "world as dream" idea quite freely. Ramaṇa Maharṣi uses the "world as dream" idea to generate the possibility that the universe is not external to us. In these exchanges M stands for Maharṣi and D for the devotee.

> M.: Are you in the world? Or is the world in you?
>
> D.: I do not understand. The world is certainly around me.
>
> M.: You speak of the world and happenings in it. They are mere ideas in you. The ideas are in the mind. The mind is within you. And so, the world is within you.
>
> D.: I do not follow you. Even if I do not think of the world, the world is still there.
>
> M.: Do you mean to say that the world is apart from the mind and it can exist in the absence of the mind?
>
> D.: Yes.
>
> M.: Does the world exist in your deep sleep?
>
> D.: It does.
>
> M.: Do you see it in your sleep?
>
> D.: No, I don't. But others, who are awake, see it.
>
> M.: Are you so aware in your sleep? Or do you become aware of the other's knowledge now?
>
> D.: In my waking state.
>
> M.: So, you speak of waking knowledge and not of sleep-experience. The existence of the world in your waking and dream states is admitted because they are the products of

27. See David Godman, ed., *op. cit.*, pp. 189-190.
28. Modern Western philosophical reflection on dreams will be pursued later in another context.

> the mind. The mind is withdrawn in sleep and the world is in the condition of a seed. It becomes manifest over again when you wake up. The ego springs forth, identifies itself with the body and sees the world. So, the world is a mental creation.
>
> D.: How can it be?
>
> M.: Do you not create a world in your dream? The waking state also is a long-drawn-out dream.[29]

This point is elaborated in greater detail in the following passage:

> Again, consider a man who dreams. He goes to sleep in a room with doors closed so that nothing can intrude on him while asleep. He closes his eyes when sleeping so that he does not see any object. Yet when he dreams, he sees a whole region in which people live and move about with himself among them. Did this panorama get in through the doors? It was simply unfolded to him by his brain. Is it the sleeper's brain? How does it hold this vast country in its tiny cells? This must explain the oft-repeated statement that the whole universe is a mere thought or a series of thoughts.[30]

Ramaṇa also uses the dream metaphor because it possesses a certain advantage over others in explicating his particular point that the world is really in us, contrary to the common belief that we are in it:

> The mirror reflects objects; yet they are not real because they cannot remain apart from the mirror. Similarly, the world is said to be a reflection in the mind as it does not remain in the absence of mind. The question arises: if the universe is a reflection, there must be a real object known as the universe

---

29. *Talks with Sri Ramaṇa Maharṣi*, p. 466. M.=Maharṣi; Devotee = questioner.

30. *Ibid.*, p. 427.

in order that it might be reflected in the mind. This amounts to an admission of the existence of an objective universe. Truly speaking, it is not so.

Therefore, the dream illustration is set forth. The dream world has no objective existence. How then is it created? Some mental impressions should be admitted. They are called *vāsanās*. How were the *vāsanās* in the mind? The answer is: they were subtle. Just as a whole tree is contained potentially in a seed, so the world is in the mind.

Then it is asked: A seed is the product of the tree which must have existed once in order that it may be reproduced. So, the world also must have been there some time. The answer is, No! There must have been several incarnations to gather the impressions which are remanifested in the present form. I must have existed before as I do now. The straight way to find an answer will be to see if the world is there. Admitting the existence of the world, I must admit a seer who is no other than myself. Let me find myself so that I may know the relation between the world and the seer. When I seek the Self and abide as the Self there is no world to be seen. What is the Reality then? The seer only and certainly not the world.

Such being the truth, the man continues to argue on the basis of the reality of the world. Whoever asked him to accept a brief for the world?[31]

Śrī Nisargadatta Mahārāj employs the "world as dream" idea even more explicitly. A questioner challenged Nisargadatta by commenting: "Your reduction of everything to dream disregards the difference between the dream of the insect and the dream of a poet. All is dream granted. But not all is equal." The ensuing discussion unfolded as follows:

31. *Ibid.*, pp. 412-13.

Mahārāj: The dreams are not equal, but the dreamer is one. I am the insect. I am the poet — in dreams. But in reality, I am neither. I am beyond all dreams. I am the light in which all dreams appear and disappear. I am both inside and outside the dream. Just like a man having a headache knows the ache and also knows that he is not the ache, so do I know the dream, myself dreaming and myself not dreaming — all at the same time. I am what I am before, during and after the dream. But what I see in dreams I am not.

Question: It is all a matter of imagination. One imagines one is dreaming, one imagines one is not dreaming. Are not both the same?

Mahārāj: The same and not the same. Not dreaming as an interval between two dreams is, of course, a part of dreaming. Not dreaming as a steady hold on and timeless abidance in reality has nothing to do with dreaming. In that sense, I never dream nor ever shall.

Question: If both dream and escape from dream are imaginings, what is the way out?

Maharaj: There is no need of a way out! Don't you see that a way out is also a part of the dream? All you have to do is to see the dream as a dream.

Question: If I start the practice of dismissing everything as a dream, where will it lead me?

Mahārāj: Wherever it leads you, it will be a dream. The very idea of going beyond the dream is illusory. Why go anywhere? Just realise that you are dreaming a dream you call the world and stop looking for ways out. The dream is not your problem. Your problem is that you like one part of your dream and not another. Love all or none of it and stop complaining. When you have seen the dream as a dream, you have done all that needs to be done.[32]

---

32. Maurice Frydman, tr., *op. cit.*, Part I, pp. 134-35.

In a way, the logical positivist assessment of dreaming as expressed by A.J. Ayer: "we do not dream but only wake up with delusive memories of experience we have never had"[33] plays right into the hands of the most uncompromising formulation of Advaita Vedānta known as *ajātivāda*. For instance, it can be argued that by taking the view of dreams Ayer does, Ayer demonstrates that "illustrations which are given in order to show that the reality is non-dual (advaita) . . . may be used for teaching the truth of non-origination (*ajāti*) also"[34] in the following way: "On the analogy of dreams, it was demonstrated that the world of waking is non-real. If it is non-real, it is un-originated. And what is left behind as the inalienable reality, viz. the self, is by its very nature unborn. Just as the snake is not at any time born of the rope, just as the *gandharvanagara* does not come into existence being duly created by an architect, just as the *māyā*-elephant is not really generated, and just as the fiery designs are not truly formed from the moving firebrand, the things of the world are not, in truth, created. The apparent birth and death of beings are illusory like the appearance and disappearance of the creatures that are formed of dreams, or made through magic (*māyāmaya*) or super-normal power (*nirmitaka*).[35]

---

33. Quoted in A.R. Manser, *op. cit.*, p. 416.

34. T.M.P. Mahādevan, *Gauḍapāda: A Study in Early Advaita*, p. 150.

35. *Ibid.*, pp. 150-51. There is a somewhat similar if startling conclusion drawn by Ramaṇa even on the basis of the waking state experience in keeping with his view that the ego does not really exist and that the illusion itself is illusory: "Whatever you see happening in the waking state happens only to the knower, and since the knower is unreal, nothing in fact ever happens" (David Godman, ed., *op. cit.*, p. 191).

4

The Uses of the Dream-Metaphor in Advaita Vedānta: Ramaṇa Maharṣi

How does the use of dream metaphor promote a better understanding of some key concepts of Advaita especially in the neo-Advaitin formulations of Advaita?

In Advaita, as in most of Hindu and even Indian thought, the world is regarded as without a beginning (*anādi*).[1] Further, this universe or the "phenomenal world is *māyā*, and it is produced by *māyā*"[2] and this "*māyā* is beginningless (*anādi*)."[3] The *jīva*[4] as well as *karma* are also beginningless (*anādi*).[5]

What are we to make of this?

In terms of the world, and of the *māyā*, the standard line has been to say:

> It is not possible to say when the world appearance began. Its origin is beyond our comprehension; for, we are subject to this

1. S. Radhakrishnan, tr., *The Brahma Sūtra*, London: George Allen & Unwin Ltd., 1960, p. 233.
2. Eliot Deutsch, *Advaita Vedānta: A Philosophical Reconstruction*, Honolulu: East-West Center Press, 1969, p. 31.
3. *Ibid.*, p. 29.
4. R. Balsubramaniam, *Advaita Vedānta*, University of Madras (Chennai), 1976, p. 209.
5. M. Hiriyanna, *The Essentials of Indian Philosophy*, pp. 45-48.

> *māyā. The child cannot be present at the birth of its mother.* We must transcend *māyā* to know its origin. This can be done only by samyakjñāna or true knowledge of Brahman. When that is attained, *māyā* is liquidated and there will be no occasion to discuss its origin. Hence, *māyā* is beginningless (*anādi*). No beginning can be postulated for it by us who are bound by it. But, though *māyā* is *anādi*, it is not ananta, without an end. *Māyā* can be annulled by Brahmajñāna which is synonymous with the realization of *Brahman* upon which the magic show of the phenomenal world will disappear.[6]

Similarly, like *māyā*, *avidyā* or individuated ignorance, which is responsible for both *jīva* and *karma*, is also *anādi*, when the "finite adjunct of the individual self is sometimes designated as *avidyā* in contrast to the cosmic *māyā* of qualified *Brahman*."[7] It is clear that the traditional explanations are functioning at two levels here: the metaphysical and the logical. We have not invoked the mythological explanation which explains the beginninglessness in the sense "a beginningless series of like things is" on the pattern of an eternal cyclical universe. That would constitute a third level. To revert now to the metaphysical: although it is couched in terms of traditional teaching, it is the logical element in it which is intriguing. Thus, if all beginnings are in time, how can time have a beginning? Kant's antinomies may be invoked in this context that one could prove "both that the world has a beginning in time and that it has no beginning in time" and that "the only way to avoid these antinomies, in Kant's opinion, is to adopt his own (critical) point of view and recognize that the world that is the object of our knowledge is a world of appearances, existing

---

6. P. Sankaranarayanan, *op. cit.*, pp. 58-59.
7. M. Hiriyanna, *Essentials of Indian Philosophy*, p. 163.

only insofar as it is constructed . . . [and as such] it is neither finite nor infinite but indefinitely extensible so neither has nor lacks a limit in space and time."[8] Is one reminded of the story from *Tripurā-Rahasya* here? A *logical* explanation of the beginningless of *jīva* and *karma* can also be offered as distinguished from the temporal. Thus, in clarifying the doctrine of *karma,* M. Hiriyanna writes:

> Here, no doubt, a question *will be asked as to when the responsibility for what one does was first incurred.* But such a question is really inadmissible, for it takes for granted that there was a time when the self was without any disposition whatsoever. Such a view of the self is an abstraction as meaningless as that of mere disposition which characterizes no one. The self, as ordinarily known to us, always means a self with a certain stock of dispositions; and this fact is indicated in Indian expositions by describing *karma* as beginningless (*anādi*). It means that no matter how far back we trace the history of an individual, we shall never arrive at a stage when he was devoid of all character.[9]

A metaphysical explanation, as distinguished from the logical, is offered in terms of the dream experience. A person has had a long day and has now fallen asleep. In due course, while asleep, the person begins to dream. Now the question to be asked is: once the person has commenced dreaming, is it possible for the person to know *in the dream* when the dream began? *In* the dream, one can keep track of the time through a dream clock but one cannot say, in terms of dream time, when the dream began, for the beginning itself is part of the dream. In this sense, clearly the dream is *anādi* and by analogy, the

---

8. W.H. Walsh, "Immanuel Kant" in Paul Edwards, Editor in Chief, *op. cit.*, Volume Four, p. 316.
9. M. Hiriyanna, *The Essentials of Indian Philosophy*, pp. 367-68.

universe. Similarly, the inherent creativity which gives rise to dreams, as well as the dream, may be called *māyā*. In that case, this *māyā* is also *anādi*, being coterminous with its beginning which is also within time, which is itself an aspect of *māyā*! In the same way, the person who appears in his or her dream — the dream-person — is also *anādi* both in the aforementioned sense as well as in the sense that the dream-person already appears as a person, that is, a karmically defined being!

Advaitic etiology contains a curiosity which the dream metaphor seems to render more accessible to understanding. In Advaita, time is "regarded as an offshoot of *māyā* and the first object to be created, so that the Advaitin does not place time and space on the same footing. Its conception presupposes the principle of causation already at work, but not so the conception of time. While all things born, excepting space, are in time and space, space is in time only. *Jīva, Īśvara* and *Māyā* are neither in time nor in space."[10]

The key point to note here, to start with, is that time precedes space. This point becomes clear when related to the dream-metaphor. Only once the dream has *started* does the mental space in which it is enacted emerge. In fact, it is not strictly true to say that it is enacted in the mental space — for the emergence of space is itself part and parcel of the enactment. Now the person who is seeing the dream, the Lord of the dream who may be postulated as its author or operator and his skills which make the dream possible — are all prior to the dream, should the situation be understood in these terms.

---

10. M. Hiriyanna, *Outlines of Indian Philosophy*, Bombay (Mumbai): Blackie & Son Publishers Private Limited, 1983, pp. 367-68.

This leads to an interesting point in Advaitic thought. Eliot Deutsch has pointed out that in some contexts, the concept of *Īśvara* or God in Advaita is "problematic. Theoretically, it would seem that the doctrine of *māyā* as a "concealing" and "distorting" power can account for appearance, as far as it can be accounted for, without the need for *Īśvara* as an explanatory concept; especially since it is maintained that the "existence" of *Īśvara* as such cannot be demonstrated rationally."[11] The dream metaphor helps clarify the problem. Once we are witnessing a dream, is it necessary to postulate a Lord of the dream who masterminds it? In terms of hermeneutical economy, it is enough to postulate a power which brings the dream into being and someone whose dream it is — the *jīva* (while the Reality slumbers!), there is no particular need to posit an *Īśvara*. It is enough to say: there is a Dream dreaming us!

However, once "whether seen as a theoretical necessity or as a practical necessity,"[12] *Īśvara* is posited, the dream metaphor *helps* to promote an understanding of the role of God in Advaita. Only now one must look upon the world as the lucid dream of God for "by hypothesis whatever is, is known to *Īśvara* and no part of it lasts longer than the time during which it is experienced. In this sense, *Īśvara* may be described as an external dreamer."[13]

Once *Īśvara* or God has been accepted in the system, once again the dream-metaphor acquires explanatory powers in relation to God. One big issue in theism is that of theodicy. But let us now for a moment revert to our daily dreams and ask: are we at all responsible for what we do or what happens

11. Eliot Deutsch, *op. cit.*, p. 43.
12. *Ibid.*, p. 38.
13. M. Hiriyanna, *Outlines of Indian Philosophy*, p. 367.

in a dream? Then if the difference between our dream and the cosmic dream of God is only one of scale, is God to be held responsible for what we do or what happens in a dream? Now one begins to understand the concept of *līlā* or sport; and the universe can similarly be regarded as the sport of God. The point to note here especially is that, compared to the activities performed in the waking state, the activities performed in a dream are non-volitional. Even the decision to play a *sport* in the waking state may be regarded as volitional; whereas even a decision to work seriously in a dream is non-volutional and hence in sport. Now one is perhaps better equipped to grasp the Advaitic concept of *līlā*:

> The concept of *līlā*, of play or sport, seeks to convey that *Īśvara* creates (sustains and destroys) worlds out of the sheer joy of doing so. Answering to no compelling necessity, his creative act is simply a release of energy for its own sake. Creation is not informed by any selfish motive. It is spontaneous, without any purpose. No moral consequences attach to the creator in his activity, for *līlā* is precisely different in kind from all action which yields results that are binding upon, and which determine, the actor. It is simply the Divine's nature to create just as it is man's nature to breathe in and out. *Līlā* thus removes all motive, purpose, and responsibility from *Īśvara* in his creative activity. Having no need to create and having no consequences attached to his action, *Īśvara* cannot be held responsible for the actions that arise subsequently within the fields of his creation. *Līlā* avoids thereby any problem of evil of the sort associated with Judaeo-Christian theism, and it sets aside as meaningless any question of why *Īśvara* creates in the first place. There can be no "why" to creation.[14]

14. Eliot Deutsch, *op. cit.*, pp. 38-39.

There is no "why" to creation, just as there is no "why" to a dream. Dr. Freud might object but the point is not just "why" there should be dreaming at all but "why" should there be this particular dream. The *fact* of a dream may be subject of speculation prior to dreaming but the *content* of the dream is analyzable only after it, even in terms of our normal living. Moreover, one is not speaking here of pathological dreams. Perhaps it is more to the point to regard the dream as an extension, an expansion of the person, a parallel, which renders Śaṅkara's remark: "Those who think about creation (*sṛṣṭi*), think that creation is the expansion of *Īśvara*"[15] more appropriate than one might otherwise feel to be the case. Two other aspects of our normal dreams may now be identified which are potentially clarificatory of Advaitic philosophy. One of them is this: in a dream, every dream-object — inert or alive — or if alive, animal or human — and if human — friend or foe — as well as oneself, and anything else in whatever form or shape — all enjoy the same ontological status. A clump of grass in the dream, qua dream object, is identical with the loveliest damsel one can dream of. This helps to convey some understanding of the state of the Realised being in Advaita, who has realised the world as a dream. Hence one encounters passages such as these: "Does a man who sees many individuals in his dream persist in believing them to be real and enquire after them when he wakes up?"[16] "From the point of the *mukta* their contention amounts to this: a man dreams a dream in which he finds several persons. On waking up, he asks: "Have the dream individuals also wakened? How ridiculous."[17] "When a man dreams, he creates himself (i.e. the *ahaṁkāra*,

15. See Eliot Deutsch, *op. cit.*, p. 38.

16. *Talks with Śrī Ramaṇa Maharṣi*, p. 530.

17. *Ibid.*, p. 478.

the seer) and the surroundings, all of them are later withdrawn into himself. The one becomes many, along with the seer."[18]

It also helps to explain the emphasis placed in the spiritual disciple or *sādhanā* of Advaita on seeing everything as one and equal. One is thus exhorted to look upon everything in the world as possessing the same value, as nothing in it possesses *objective* value. "Therefore, the dream illustration is set forth. The dream world has no objective existence:"[19]

> A dreamer dreams a dream. He sees the *dream* world with pleasures, pains, etc. But he wakes up and then loses all interest in the dream world. So it is with the waking world also. Just as the dream-world, being only a part of yourself and not different from you, ceases to interest you, so also the present world would cease to interest you if you awake from this waking dream (saṁsāra) and realise that it is a part of yourself, and not an objective reality. Because you think that you are apart from the objects around you, you desire a thing. But, if you understand that the thing was only a thought-form you would no longer desire it.[20]

The second aspect worth remarking is the fact that while one was dreaming, suppose someone came and told one in one's dream that one is dreaming and that one is really not what one appears to be in the dream, and that one's dream-body is not one's real form. What would such statements amount to? The point is worth pursuing because it replicates our existential situation. We live in this apparently real world and never doubt its verity until exposed to some form of thought, which generates the possibility that this world whose reality we take for granted *may* be a dream-world. Should this idea gain a

18. *Ibid.*, p. 451.
19. *Ibid.*, p. 413.
20. *Ibid.*, p. 588.

measure of plausibility in our minds, what can we presume to know now about ourselves which we did not know before?

A little reflection yields the striking conclusion that if such be the case, then we *know what we are not but do not know what we are*. Let us imagine that a king goes to sleep and dreams that he is a beggar. In that dream, he is then accosted by a student who has just taken a course in Advaita Vedānta. And when the beggar approaches him to have his palm greeted by a few dollars, the impecunious donor tells him that he has no dollars to offer, but can offer an insight which far exceeds the value of money. The poor beggar, let us assume, has developed the required receptivity to spiritual instruction as a consequence of his exposure to destitution on account of the introspection known to accompany it. The student now tells the beggar in the dream: "Here's a priceless penny of Hindu wisdom. This whole world is a dream." Now if the beggar were to put faith in this statement, what would he now know about himself that he did not know before? He would know that he is *not* really a beggar; but he would not know who he really is until he wakes up.

This is the predicament in which the votaries of Advaita find themselves, which necessitates the use of *via negativa* in religious discourse. Just as all one can say of oneself in the dream is: "I am not this, I am not this." — *neti neti* and one cannot affirm what one is because one is still dreaming; just as all the beggar can say in the dream is "I am not a beggar, but what I am I know not," similarly the scriptural texts can only tell us in our dream-world that the reality is not this, not this — what it is we have to realise for ourselves. A sage is then like a day-dreamer who has penetrated into our dream — who can tell us who are dreaming what it might be like to be awake.

This point is of some significance, as usually the expression *neti neti* is taken as a description or rather the denial of the description of Brahman but in point of fact, it is far more often applied to *ātman* in the actual texts where it occurs. The philosophical argument in favour of *ātman* in any case, is clearly illuminated by the dream-metaphor:

> Do you understand that you cannot ask a valid question about yourself, because you do not know whom you are asking about. In the question, "Who am I?" the "I" is not known and the question can be worded as: "I do not know what I mean by "I"." What you are, you must find out. *I can only tell you what you are not. You are not of the world, you are not even in the world. The world is not, you alone are. You create the world in your imagination like a dream. As you cannot separate the dream from yourself, so you cannot have an outer world independent of yourself. You are independent, not the world. Don't be afraid of a world you yourself have created. Cease from looking for happiness and reality in a dream and you will wake up.* You need not know all the "why" and "how," there is no end to questions. Abandon all desires, keep your mind silent and you shall discover.[21]

Advaita also makes the initially startling claim, as noted earlier, that one is not in the universe as one presumes to be the case, rather the universe is in oneself. The dream-metaphor again helps clarify the point. While our dream-bodies may be part of the dream and within it, the whole dream is *in* the recumbent sleeper along with the dream-body. As Ramaṇa remarks: "You dream of finding yourself in another town. Can another town enter your room? Could you have left and gone there? Both are possible. Both are unreal. They appear real to the mind. The "I" of the dream has vanished. But the

---

21. Maurice Frydman, tr., *op. cit.*, pp. 452-53, emphasis added.

substratum of the mind continues all along. Find that and you will be happy."[22]

Ramaṇa and Nisargadatta make frequent use of the dream-metaphor to illustrate their points. Ramaṇa is even inclined to lump *both* the waking and dream states as nothing more than dream, a step Śaṅkara might hesitate to take. Says Ramaṇa:

> All that we see is dream, whether we see it in the dream state or waking state. On account of some arbitrary standards about the duration of the experience and so on, we call one experience a dream and another waking experience. With reference to reality both the experiences are unreal. A man might have such an experience as getting *anugraha* (grace) in his dream and the effects and influence of it on his entire subsequent life may be so profound and so abiding that one cannot call it unreal, while calling real some trifling incident in the waking life that just flits by, is casual and of no moment and is soon forgotten. Once I had an experience, a vision or a dream, whatever you may call it. I and some others including Chadwick had a walk on the hill. Returning we were walking along a huge street with great buildings on either side. Showing the street and buildings, I asked Chadwick and others whether anybody could say that what we were seeing was a dream and they all replied, "Which fool will say so?" and we walked along and entered the hall and the vision or dream ceased, or woke up. What are we to call this?[23]

In fact, Ramaṇa even compares the process of Realization to a dream-sequence:

---

22. Paul Brunton and Munagala Venkataramiah, *Conscious Immortality*, Tiruvannāmalai: Śrī Ramaṇasramam, 1984, pp. 98-99.
23. A. Devaraja Mudaliar, *Gems from Bhagavan*, Triuvannāmalai: Sri Ramaṇāsramam, 1978, pp. 24-25.

> Our real nature is *mukti*. But we are imagining that we are bound and are making various strenuous attempts to become free, while we are all the time free. This will be understood only when we reach that stage. We will be surprised that we frantically were trying to attain something which we have always been and are. An illustration will make this clear. A man goes to sleep in this hall. He dreams he has gone on a world tour, is roaming over the hill and dale, forest and country, desert and sea, across various continents and, after many years of weary and strenuous travel, returns to this country, reaches Tiruvannāmalai, enters the Āśramam and walks into the hall. Just at that moment he wakes up and finds he has not moved an inch, but was sleeping where he lay down. He has not returned after great effort to the hall but is and always has been in the hall. It is exactly like that. If it is asked why being free we imagine we are bound, I answer, "Why being in the hall did you imagine you were on a world adventure, crossing hill and dale, desert and sea?" It is all mind or *māyā*.[24]

The basic function of the dream-metaphor is to establish the possible illusoriness of the experience of the waking state which we take for granted as real. This is established in at least four ways: logically, phenomenologically, psychologically and analogically. It is the last which will concern us the most but the other approaches are also not without interest. One can always rely on Śaṅkara to present the logical argument:

> Śaṅkara puts the argument in the form of a five-membered syllogism: the things seen in waking are illusory (*pratijñā*); because they are seen (*hetu*); like the things seen in dream (*dṛṣṭānta*); as in dream there is illusoriness for the things seen, so even in waking the characteristic of being seen is

24. *Ibid.*, pp. 34-35.

> the same (*hetūpanaya*); therefore, even in waking the illusoriness of things is declared (*nigamana*).[25]

The phenomenological argument turns on the point that the objects, whether in dreaming or waking essentially "appear" in that state. But unlike Husserl, the Advaitins are not attached to the appearance as such:

> Another reason for classing the world of waking with the contents of dream is that it is also evanescent. What is non-existent in the beginning and at the end, is so even in the present. That is real which is not conditioned by time. Per contra that which is conditioned by time cannot be real. Just as the dream-objects are experienced in dream alone, neither before nor after, even so the objects of waking are experienced in the state of waking alone.[26]

The psychological argument ultimately rests on the common denominator constituted by the mind in the experiences of both waking and dreaming. Thus Ramaṇa says: "In waking state, ego identifies itself with the physical body; in dreaming with subtle mind"[27] but, for Ramaṇa, ego and the mind are the same.[28] And "it might be laid down as a rule *that whatever is seen by the mind is void of Reality*."[29] How does one arrive at such a conclusion? It may be argued that what is seen by the mind in a dream is void of reality. This of course does not by itself establish the fact that all that is seen by the mind is like a dream and void of reality but constitutes an important premise in the argument as it is developed. Thus Gauḍapāda:

---

25. T.M.P. Mahadevan, *Gauḍapāda: A Study in Early Advaita*, p. 122.
26. T.M.P. Mahadevan *Gauḍapāda: A Study in Early Advaita*, p. 122.
27. Paul Brunton and Munagala Venkataramiah, p. 101.
28. *Talks with Śrī Ramaṇa Maharṣi*, p. 396.
29. T.M.P. Mahadevan *Gauḍapāda: A Study in Early Advaita*, p. 121, emphasis added.

> starts with the premise that the objects seen in dream are illusory. The dreamer sees things like the mountain and the elephant in his phantasy. But judged by the measure of waking space, these, had they been real, must have been present within the body, which is impossible. How could the huge objects seen in dream be contained within the confined space of the body? If any location could be assigned to the dream-contents from the standpoint of waking, it must be the body. But the absurdity in assigning a limited space to things that cannot be contained in it is too patent to require any explanation. It may be held that the dreamer sees things not within the body but in their respective places as he would see them in waking. But such contention will not bear a moment's scrutiny. In a trice of waking time one may travel far and wide in dream. If one were really to go to those places, it would take a long time. And moreover if the dreamer actually goes to the place of which he dreamed, he must wake up there and not at the place where he had been sleeping.[30]

Now the question arises — why are objects not real when they appear to be so in the dream. They are not so because they do not appear as real *in the waking world*; because:

> The dreams do not conform to the laws of space and time which govern the waking world. In a dream that lasts but for a few moments, one might imagine to have lived through centuries or gone round the world many times over. The *things* experienced in dream are not real for the reason that they are not seen on waking. One might dream of friends and of talking with them; but when the dream spell is broken one does not find them. The things that the dreamer might receive in his dreams he does not see to remain in his possession when he wakes. The *body* which appears to roam about in dream is unreal, because distinct from it there is

30. *Ibid.*, pp. 120-21.

> another body seen in the place where the dreamer lies. The dream-body is really a figment of the mind. As is the body, so are all the objects perceived in dream illusory. It may be laid down as a rule, then, that whatever is seen by the mind is void of reality.[31]

The point then is that "the objects of waking are perceived as the dream-contents are; and whatever is perceived is illusory." But is this not a non-sequitur? In ordinary experience we may occasionally perceive imaginary objects, but usually perceive actual objects. For instance, the waking world can be distinguished from the dream world on the following grounds: (1) that the objects experienced in the waking state are practically efficient — one can use the actual chair in a way one can't use the dream chair; (2) dreams are strange and abnormal; (3) in waking state we are aware we are awake but not in a dream that we are dreaming; (4) dreams take place within the body, the waking state involves the outside world; (5) the dream objects are hazy, of the waking world manifest; (6) dream-objects last only as long as the dream lasts but waking life objects are perceived before and after the dream.

T.M.P. Mahadevan represents Gauḍapāda as rejecting the first three of this set of six arguments and accepting the last three because the "*empirical difference* between waking and dream is not denied by Gauḍapāda."[32] It seems however that all the six arguments are capable of being refuted. I shall try to refute the first two following Mahadevan, the third and fourth following Ramaṇa and shall offer my own refutation for the last two.

Argument 1: that objects in the waking state are practically more efficient:

---

31. *Ibid.*, p. 121.

32. *Ibid.*, p. 125, emphasis added.

> A difference between the two states cannot be made out on the ground that, while the objects experienced in waking are *practically efficient*, those seen in dream are not; for even the objects of waking experience are fruitful in practice only in that state and not in dream; and the dream-objects are useful in their own way in the state of dream. It is true that the dream-water cannot quench actual thirst. But it is equally true that the so-called actual water cannot quench the dream thirst. A man may eat and drink and feel quite satisfied in his waking state. But at the next moment he may go to sleep and dream that he is racked with hunger and thirst and feel as if he had not had food and drink for days and nights. The contrary may also happen. A man satisfied with food and drink in dream may find himself, on waking, extremely hungry and thirsty. Thus it cannot be said that the things of the waking world alone are fruitful or practically efficient. If they "work" in waking, the dream-contents "work" in dream.[33]

Argument 2: That dreams are strange and abnormal. This argument is countenanced by Śaṅkara when he comments on *Brahma-Sūtra* 3.2.3.[34] T.M.P. Mahadevan notes:

> It may be argued that, since the contents of dream are quite different from the objects of waking, they cannot constitute the illustration for proving the illusoriness of the waking world. The dream-*contents* are strange and abnormal, and are not the replica of what are experienced in waking. It has been said that the things seen in dream are strange and abnormal. But when and to whom do they appear abnormal? To him who has returned to waking after a dream. In the dream state itself the contents are not realised to be strange.

33. *Ibid.*, pp. 122-23.

34. William M. Indich, *Consciousness in Advaita Vedānta*, p. 63.

> It is from the side of waking that the dream-contents seem abnormal; but in themselves they are quite normal.[35]

And, further, relying on Śaṅkara's comments on Gauḍapāda-kārikā II.8, Mahadevan adds:

> Just as a traveller who is well-instructed goes to a place and sees there strange things which are but natural to that place, so the dreamer transported as he is to the dream-world experiences strange things. Each state or circumstance has its own peculiarity. But that cannot prevent comparison of the waking-world with the *contents* of dream.[36]

Argument 3: We are aware that we are awake, but not aware that we are dreaming when dreaming. This is so because the objects are external to us in the waking state, whereas they *appear* within us upon waking. For as soon as one wakes from the dream one realises the "unreality of even the things he saw in the dream *as if* outside." The point made by Realised Advaitins like Ramaṇa is that just as on *waking* alone one realises the objects which seemed external were within the dream, upon Realization it dawns on one that the objects of the world one sees outside were really within us. In other words, the experience of the waking state after the awakening is the reverse of the experience of the dreaming state in the waking state. In this way, the two states — waking and dreaming, are rendered not less but more compatible!

Argument 4: Dream states are within the body, waking state experiences outside it. The previous counterargument flows over into this one, but let us examine the objection as it stands. Thus it is said "that in dream there is no physical object which we cognize; but in waking life there is a physical object.

35. T.M.P. Mahadevan, *Gauḍapāda: A Study in Early Advaita*, pp. 123-24.

36. *Ibid.*, p. 124.

How do you know there is a table or a ball in waking life? Your information is by the interpretation of sense impressions in a dream. The feeling that there is an object external to oneself is common both to waking and to dream life."[37] If it be maintained that in waking state the object is actually external and in dream state only seemingly so, then it needs to be recognized that this statement about the dream state is being made from within the waking state. What, one would want to know, would be a description of the waking state read like when made from within the dream state?

Argument 5: This is best expressed in terms of *Brahma-Sūtra* 3.2.3: "The dream is only an illusion; for its nature is not completely manifest"[38] compared to waking. Dreams are known to be sometimes quite vivid and lucid, and perception in the waking state is not always on target. But these are superficial responses compared to the main one — that the nature of the equipment in relation to the environment determines the quality of perception. In dreams the senses function unaided with sense organs; and one can see how different the waking world appears, when sense organs function aided by sensory extensions such as telescope and microscope. Hence not only is difference between dreaming and waking one of clarity or otherwise; it is of degree rather than of kind and in keeping with the overall context as in dreaming "the external senses are inactive, and in the cognition" of waking state "they function." It may even be argued that dreams disclose matter as it really is — permeable and malleable — like iron ore — before it is cast into a metallic object by the external senses!

---

37. P. Sankaranarayanan, *op. cit.*, p. 45.
38. *Ibid.* Also see Swami Gambhirananda, tr., *Brahma-Sūtra-bhāṣya of Śrī Śaṅkarācārya,* Calcutta (Kolkata): Advaita Ashrama, 1965, pp. 591-92.

Argument 6: Dream objects last for the duration of the dream but waking objects outlast dream objects. Three counter-arguments may be urged in consideration here. (1) Waking state objects outlast dream objects when the dream state is examined from the vantage point of the waking state. What status waking state objects have from within the dream state we do not know. (2) Dream objects last as long as the dream lasts, and waking objects last so long as the waking state lasts. In this sense there is parity. (3) A different imaginative procedure seems to yield a different result. If a person has a dream within a dream, then on waking up from his "dream" within the dream he would think he is in a waking state, as the objects would now appear external to him. Is he in one? Perhaps, but only relative to another dream state.

Stronger objections designed to question any equation between waking and dream state involve the issue of intrasubjectivity and objectivity. Several points arise in this context. (1) The objects seen in a dream are private to the dreamer. This is true even if it be argued that in a dream a public might appear: "Many people appear; they talk to each other and to the dreamer, and so, there is a like common experience,"[39] as in a waking state when people other than the dreamer see the same object. However, this community of people in the dream is from within, while those in the waking state testifying to a common object are outside the person. (2) Even when in the waking state the person ceases to experience an object, as when asleep, others testify to its continued experience. So the object is independent of the observer.

Both these arguments of naive realism, are, however, undermined if the "dream within a dream" argument is used. Another possible refutation would run as follows: "As it is

39. P. Sankaranarayanan, *op. cit.*, pp. 45-46.

possible that several men may see the same dream, it happens that we all experience the same objects."[40]

It appears, then, that the use of dreams, or rather the metaphor of the world as dream, enables the plausibility of the Advaitin world-view to be considerably enhanced; but it remains problematical. It creates the problem of "the impossibility of communication among the *jīva*s."[41] Ramaṇa seems to incline towards that very view of Advaita which must face these problems squarely. The view is generally known as *dṛṣṭi-sṛṣṭi-vāda* or the doctrine of simultaneous creation — "that the world only exists when it is perceived." Although it may "sound perverse, Śrī Ramaṇa insisted that the serious seeker should be satisfied with it, partly because it is the most beneficial attitude to adopt if one is seriously interested in realizing the self."[42] Perhaps the best way to proceed would be to first offer a statement by Ramaṇa on his own position and then to examine the manner in which he addresses the problems posed by it in the context of the doctrine that the world is like a dream.

The doctrine can be formulated in four ways as found in Ramaṇa: (1) that there are three views of creation found in Advaita and it represents one of them; (2) that three levels of truth are admitted in Advaita and it corresponds to one of them; (3) that several approaches are utilized in Advaita to demonstrate the unreality of the world and this is one of them; and (4) adopting any other doctrine of creation or another

40. B.L. Atreya, "Philosophy of the Yogavāsiṣṭha" in Haridas Bhattacharyya, ed., *The Cultural Heritage of India*, Calcutta (Kolkata): The Ramakrishna Mission Institute of Culture, 1953, Volume III, p. 428. Also see B.L. Atreya, *Yogavāsiṣṭha and Modern Thought*, Banaras: The Indian Book Shop, 1954.

41. P.T. Raju, *Idealistic Thought in Idea*, p. 104.

42. David Godman, ed., *op. cit.* p. 183.

level of truth is an accommodation or adjustment — as you will — to the ability, or in this case rather the inability, of the seeker to grasp the truth.

The following statement on the doctrine of creation in Advaita is a classic one and has often been condensed, rephrased, or cited in parts or in full. It is cited in toto here:

> The *ajāta* school of Advaita says, "Nothing exists except the one reality. There is no birth or death, no projection or drawing in, no *sādhaka* (practiser), no *mumukṣu* (one who desires to be liberated), no *mukta* (one who is liberated), no bondage, no liberation. The one unity alone exists for ever." To such that find it difficult to grasp this truth and ask, "How can we ignore this solid world we see all around us?" the dream experience is pointed out and they are told, "All that you see depends on the seen." This is called *dṛṣṭi-sṛṣṭi-vāda* or the argument that one first creates out of his mind and then sees what his mind itself has created.
>
> To such that cannot grasp even this and who further argue: "The dream experience is so short, while the world always exists. The dream experience was limited to me. But the world is felt and seen not only by me but by so many and we cannot call such a world non-existent," the argument called *sṛṣṭi-dṛṣṭi-vāda* is addressed and they are told, "God first created such and such a thing out of such and such an element and then something else and so forth." That alone will satisfy them. Their mind is not otherwise satisfied and they ask themselves "How can all geography, all maps, all sciences, stars, planets and the rules governing or relating to them, and all knowledge be totally untrue?" To such it is best to say: "Yes. God created all this and so you see it." All these are only to suit the capacity of the hearers. The absolute can only be one.[43]

43. A. Devaraja Mudaliar, compiler, *Gems From Bhagavān*, Triuvannamālai: Śrī Ramaṇasramam, 1978, pp. 3-4.

Curiously, the metaphor of the world as dream arises either directly or by implication in the context of all the theories. The most direct example of this is offered by an illustration of the *dṛṣṭi-sṛṣṭi-vāda* as in the following passage:

There are three methods of approach in Advaita-*vāda*.

(1) The *ajātavāda* is represented by no loss, no creation, no one bound, no *sādhaka*, no one desirous of liberation, no liberation. This is the Supreme Truth. (*Māṇḍukya Kārikā*, II-32).

According to this, there is only One and it admits of no discussion.

(2) *Dṛṣṭi-Sṛṣṭi-vāda* is illustrated thus:- Simultaneous creation. There are two friends sleeping side by side. One of them *dreams* that he goes to Benares with his friends and returns. He tells his friend that both of them have been to Benares. The other denies it. That statement is true from the standpoint of one and the denial from that of the other.

(3) *Dṛṣṭi-Sṛṣṭi-vāda* is plain (Gradual creation and knowledge of it).[44]

But it has also been pressed in use in the context of *ajātavāda* by at least the followers of Ramaṇa, as in the situation of looking at the world from the *ajñānī*'s point of view.

> The *ajñānī*, on the other hand, is totally unaware of the unitary nature and source of the world and, as a consequence, his mind constructs an illusory world of separate interacting objects by persistently misinterpreting the sense-impressions it receives. Śrī Ramaṇa pointed out that this view of the world has no more reality than a dream since it superimposes a creation of the mind on the reality of

44. *Talks with Śrī Ramaṇa Maharṣi*, pp. 348-49.

> the Self. He summarized the difference between the *jñānī*'s and the *ajñānī*'s standpoint by saying that the world is unreal if it is perceived by the mind as a collection of discrete objects and real when it is directly experienced as an appearance in the Self.[45]

In the case of the *dṛṣṭi-sṛṣṭi-vāda*, or creation as the creation of God, or *Īśvarasṛṣṭi* in formal Advaita, the world can be viewed as God's dream.[46] Ramaṇa often depicts "the world to be God"[47] or advises: "You should certainly keep God in your mind for seeing God all around you"[48] in the context of spiritual praxis, but is less forthcoming in using the metaphor of the world as dream in relation to God. When such a point is approached in discussion with a questioner the point is left unresolved:

> M.: *Saṁskāra (predisposition) is saṁsāra (cycle of births and deaths).*
>
> D.: Right. *All this is Vāsudeva* — this truth has been forgotten by us. So we cannot identify ourselves with God.
>
> M.: Where is forgetfulness?
>
> D.: Like *svapna.*
>
> M.: Whose svapna?
>
> D.: *Jīva*'s
>
> M.: Who is *jīva*?
>
> D.: It is Paramātmā's.
>
> M.: Let Paramātmā ask then.[49]

---

45. David Godman, ed., *op. cit.* p. 182.
46. M. Hiriyanna, *Outlines of Indian Philosophy*, p. 367.
47. *Talks with Śrī Ramaṇa Maharṣi*, p. 1.
48. *Ibid.*, p. 212.
49. *Ibid.*, pp. 249-50.

At another point, he commits himself more but the situation remains equivocal, when in the context of the *prātibhāsika* level, associated with dreams and illusions he says: "So there is only one *jīva*, be it the individual or God."[50]

This prepares the ground for the transition to the second approach, to the issue of *dṛṣṭi-sṛṣṭi-vāda* used by Ramaṇa, that of the three levels of reality. He says:

> As was already said, the purpose of the whole philosophy is to indicate the underlying Reality whether of the *jāgrat*, *svapna* and *suṣupti* states, or the individual souls, the world and God.

There are three possibilities involved here:

(1) The *vyāvahārika*: The man sees the world in all its variety, surmises the creator and believes in himself as the subject. All these are thus reduced to the three fundamentals, *jagat*, *jīva* and *Īśvara*. He learns the existence of the creator and tries to reach him in order to gain immortality. If one is thus released from bondage, there are all other individuals existing as before who should work out their own salvation. He more or less admits the One Reality underlying all these phenomena. The phenomena are due to the play of *māyā*. *Māyā* is the śakti of Īśvara or the activity of Reality. Thus existence of different souls, objects, etc. do not clash with the advaitic point of view.

(2) The *prātibhāsika*: The *jagat*, *jīva* and *Īśvara* are all cognised by the seer only. They do not have any existence independent of him. *So there is only one jīva, be it the individual or God.* All else is simply a myth.

50. *Ibid.*, p. 374.

(3) The *pāramārthika*: i.e., ajātavāda (no-creation doctrine) which *admits of no second*. There is no reality or absence of it, no seeking or gaining, no bondage or liberation and so on.[51]

At this point in the discourse Ramaṇa himself raises a question and in answering it uses the dream-metaphor as an illustration of all the levels, ending the discussion with a tantalizing equation of the waking and dream states, as if to imply that the *vyāvahārika* or waking state only *seems* not to share the features of dreaming:

> The question arises why then do all the *śāstras* speak of the Lord as the creator? How can the creature that you are create the creator and argue that the *jagat*, *jīva* and *Īśvara* are mental conceptions only?

The answer runs as follows:-

> You know that your father of this *jāgrat* state is dead and that several years have elapsed since his death. However you see him in your *dream* and recognise him to be your father, of whom you were born and who has left patrimony to you. Here the *creator is in the creature*. Again, you *dream* that you are serving a king and that you are a part of the administrative wheel of the kingdom. As soon as you wake up all of them have disappeared leaving you, the single individual, behind. Where were they all? Only in yourself. The same analogy holds good in the other case also.
>
> D.: In the *vyāvahārika*, above mentioned, how does *māyā* come in?
>
> M.: *Māyā* is only *Īśvara-Śakti* or the activity of Reality.
>
> D: Why does it become active?

51. *Ibid.*, pp. 373-74.

M.: How can this question arise? You are yourself within its fold. Are you standing apart from that universal activity in order to ask this question? The same Power is raising this doubt in order that all doubts may finally cease.

D.: The *dream* world is not purposeful as the *jāgrat* world, because we do not feel that wants are satisfied.

M.: You are not right. There are thirst and hunger in dream also. You might have had your fill and kept over the remaining food for the next day. Nevertheless you feel hungry in dream. This food does not help you. Your dream-hunger can be satisfied by dream-creations only.

D.: We recollect our *dream*s in our *jāgrat* but not vice versa.

M.: Not right again. In the dream you identify yourself with the one now speaking.

D.: But we do not know that we are dreaming as apart from waking as we do now.

M.: The dream is the combination of *jāgrat* and *suṣupti*. It is due to the *saṁskāra*s of the *jāgrat* state. Hence we remember dreams at present. *Saṁskāra*s are not formed contrarywise; therefore also we are not aware of the dream and *jāgrat* simultaneously. Still everyone will recollect strange perplexities in dream. One wonders, if he dreams is he awake? He argues and determines that he is only awake. When really awake, he finds that it was all only a dream.[52]

Elsewhere he is more explicit, though he does not clearly identify himself with the position. If he did, that would indeed be an avowal of the metaphor the world as dream in a very comprehensive manner:

If *Reality be used in the wider sense the world* may be said to have the everyday life and illusory degrees (*vyāvahārika* and *prātibhāsika satya*). Some, however, deny even the reality of

---

52. *Ibid.*, pp. 374-75.

> practical life — *vyāvahārika satya* and consider it to be only projection of the mind. According to them it is only *prātibhāsika satya*, i.e., an illusion.[53]

The next approach may now be considered — the one which uses the dream-metaphor to establish the *objective* unreality of the world.[54]

Indeed, the dream seems to be Ramaṇa's favourite metaphor to establish the point that "the objective world is really subjective."[55] Thus "when a man dreams, he creates himself (. . .) and his surroundings. All of them are later withdrawn into himself. The one becomes many, along with the seer. Similarly one becomes many in the waking state."[56] This passage was cited on account of its succinctness earlier. Again, when he avers that "the world is a mental creation" and his statement is met with skepticism, he remarks: "Do you not create a world in your dream? The waking state is also a long-drawn-out dream."[57] In fact Ramaṇa believes that because we are busy seeing the dream, we have lost touch with the seer and that's part of the problem if not the whole of it:

> There was a man who saw in his *dream* his father who had died thirty years earlier. Furthermore he dreamt that he had four more brothers and that his father divided his property among them. A quarrel ensued, the brothers assaulted the man and he woke up in a fright. Then he remembered that he was all alone, he had no brothers and the father was dead long ago. His fright gave place to contentment. So you

53. *Ibid.*, p. 42.
54. *Ibid.*, pp. 412-13.
55. *Ibid.*, p. 451.
56. *Ibid.*
57. *Ibid.*, p. 466.

> see — when we see our Self there is no world, and when we lose sight of the Self we get ourselves bound in the world.[58]

One last point while presenting the views of Ramaṇa remains to be clarified before the problems raised by it are tackled:

> The Vedānta says that the cosmos springs into view simultaneously with the seer. There is no detailed process of creation. This is said to be *yugapat sṛṣṭi* (instantaneous creation). It is quite similar to the creations in *dream* where the experiencer springs up simultaneously with the objects of experience. *When this is told, some people are not satisfied for they are so rooted in objective knowledge. They seek to find out how there can be sudden creation. They argue that an effect must be preceded by a cause. In short, they desire an explanation for the existence of the world which they see around them.* Then the Śrutis try to satisfy their curiosity by such theories of creation. This method of dealing with the subject of creation is called *krama sṛṣṭi* (gradual creation). But the true seeker can be content with *yugapat sṛṣṭi* — instantaneous creation.[59]

Now one is ready to face the question: if the universe is a dream, who is the dreamer? Whose dream is it? Yours, mine, God's — or are all involved in some mysterious way — or is it that we are making distinctions without difference?

Ramaṇa does not offer a precise answer but seems to point in the direction of the last one. The clue is provided by the fact that he seems to regard the multiplicity of the subjects in the dream as part of the dream. In fact he implies that even at the *empirical* level we are not *one* subject: "The "I" of the dream soon vanishes, and another "I" speaks of the dream."[60] And

58. *Ibid.*, p. 518.

59. *Ibid.*, pp. 612-13, emphasis added.

60. *Ibid.*, p. 54.

again: "Do you not have a body in your dream? Is it not different from the recumbent body on the bed?"[61]

Thus once we realise that we, despite the fact that "no one will admit of two selves in himself"[62] become at least dual subjects — in waking and dream, we will be more willing to admit the next two points about other subjects or *jīva*s which Ramaṇa makes. But a point must be clarified here lest a misunderstanding develop subsequently. Although the dream-ego or the waking-ego seem to differ, they all tie into the same one ego:

> D.: A man *dreams* of a tiger, takes fright and wakes up. The dream-tiger appears to the dream ego who is also frightened. When he wakes up how is it that that ego disappears, and the man wakes up as the waking ego?
>
> M.: That establishes that the ego is the same. Dream, wakefulness and sleep are passing phases for the *same ego*.[63]

Not only does Ramaṇa establish the same "ego," in another context he establishes the same "I" — thereby underscoring the significance of the point. In the first passage the initial moves are made in that direction; they are carried through in the next:

> In the present body you say the *dream* body is astral. Did you say so in the dream body? What is astral now would appear real then, the present body itself is astral according to that view-point. What is the difference between one astral body and another? There is no difference between the two.[64]
>
> Again consider it from another point of view: You create a dream-body for yourself in the *dream* and act with that dream-

61. *Ibid.*, p. 126.

62. *Ibid.*

63. *Ibid.*, p. 449.

64. *Ibid.*, p. 127.

> body. The same is falsified in the waking state. At present you think that you are this body and not the dream-body. So that, you see, neither of these bodies is real. Because each of them is true for a time and false at other times. That which is real must be real for ever. But you say "I." This "I" — consiousness is present all through the three states. There is no change in it. That is alone real.[65]

Two main points need to be taken into account to advance the argument further. They are contained in the following two pieces of discourse. The first has been cited earlier in full but the part of it which is relevant here has to deal with the question raised by the panorama one sees in a dream.

> Did this panorama get in through the doors? It was simply unfolded to him by his brain. *Is it the sleeper's brain or in the brain of the dream individual? It is in the sleeper's brain.* How does it hold this vast country in its tiny cells? This must explain the oft-repeated statement that the whole universe is a mere thought or a series of thoughts.[66]

The point involved, I think, is an important one. John Smith goes to sleep and dreams and also sees himself in the dream as Janet Brown. Now the dream is unfolding in the mind of John Smith. Though he himself appears in the dream as Janet Brown, it is not Janet Brown's dream. In terms of the dream-metaphor our situation in the world we live in now is that of Janet Brown, not John Smith — though in a sense they are the same.

The next point is embedded in what, on the face of it, are two very simple and short sentences: "A *jīva* is only the light reflected on the ego. The person identifies himself with the

---

65. *Ibid.*, p. 294.
66. *Ibid.*, p. 427.

ego and argues that there must be more like him. He is not easily convinced of the absurdity of his position."[67]

I think the point being made is this. Janet Brown is a figment of John Smith's imagination and so are all other individuals in the dream. They are all equally fictitious beings, but Janet Brown will find it hard to accept this. In fact all other individuals will find it hard to accept this. The *same* mental process which made John Smith appear as Janet Brown has made *everything* else appear in the dream and everybody else. Let the mental processes that caused the dream to appear be called *vāsanās*, or latent tendencies of the mind, which set the dream in motion. It should be further recognized that Janet Brown in the dream is the ego of John Smith asleep. Now perhaps the following statement of Ramaṇa can be decoded in a modern idiom: "The ego, the world and the individuals are all due to the person's *vāsanās*. When they perish, that person's hallucinations disappear."[68] Or vice versa.

The various *jīvas* or figures in the dream could also be said to result, as indeed the dream itself, from John Smith's ignorance in sleep that he is John Smith — they are the result of his *avidyā*. And should any one in the dream, be it Janet Brown or *anyone else* realise somehow that *he* or *she* is really John Smith, that person's whole perspective on the dream will be totally altered. This would amount to liberation. For this to happen, this other person, say Robert Scot, or even Janet Brown, does not have to disappear from the dream nor does the dream have to dissolve.

Now if the question is asked: whose is *avidyā*? — what does one say? What can one say? Everyone in the dream is

67. *Ibid.*, p. 530.

68. *Ibid.*, p. 530

under the influence of ignorance though it is really John Smith's ignorance of himself. But it is equally the ignorance of everyone in the dream about their real self. Looked at in this way, how do we now understand the following comments:

> Then ask, "Whose is the *avidyā*?" *Avidyā* is ignorance. It implies subject and object. Become the subject and there will be no object.
>
> D.: What is *avidyā*?
>
> M.: Ignorance of Self. Who is ignorant of the Self? The self must be ignorant of Self. Are there two selves?
>
> D.: Does Bhagavān (Ramaṇa) see the world as part and parcel of himself? How does he see the world?
>
> M.: The Self alone is and nothing else. However, it is differentiated owing to ignorance. Differentiation is threefold: (1) of the same kind: (2) of a different kind; and (3) as parts in itself. The world is not another self similar to the self. It is not different from the self; nor is it part of the self.[69]

If the threefold differentiation is applied to the self we obtain (1) John Smith and Janet Brown — of the same kind; (2) other *jīvas* in the dream, of a different kind and (3) the three egos — dream-ego, waking-ego and sleeping no-ego of John Smith, as "parts in itself."

It seems that all or any of these *could* be brought into relation to the dream as participants of the dream but there is *one* outside the dream, the dream is inside him. He is John Smith. It seems difficult to penetrate beyond this point but it is difficult not to get the impression that, given the key role assigned to *vāsanā* by Ramaṇa, he looks upon each *vāsanā*-harbouring *jīva* as dreaming his own world. This is often referred to as *dṛṣṭi-sṛṣṭi-vāda*.

---

69. *Ibid.*, p. 531.

P.T. Raju has identified three versions of the *dṛṣṭi-sṛṣṭi-vāda* theory. Perhaps if the three versions could be identified and if Ramaṇa's version could be identified with one of them, then the matter could be brought closer to resolution. Raju presents the view as follows:

(1) On one of its forms the doctrine may be summarized as follows:

According to *one form*, both ignorance, *avidyā* (*māyā*) and the world are created by the mind of the *jīva* (individual) without the help of the sense organs and their contact with external things, in the same way as, in dreams, mind creates its objects.[70]

(2) The second version is then described as an effort to accommodate to a criticism of the first:

But then the difficulty is felt of explaining how the *jīva*, who is a product of *avidyā*, can create *avidyā* through his cognitive act. Hence according to the second form of the theory, it is maintained that the world of forms but not the original *avidyā* is created by the *jīva*'s perception. This theory corresponds to Berkeley's doctrine *ese est percipi*.[71]

(3) Next a third version is identified:

There is another variant of this theory. For it, perception is not the same as creation, but is simultaneous with creation. But this view can hold true only for those *jīva*s which experience their identity with the Brahman. And it can be held only when this identity is established, that is, when the truth of the Brahman and its identity with the *jīva* are acknowledged, just

70. P.T. Raju, *op. cit.*, p. 103.

71. *Ibid.*

> as the world can be regarded as a superimposition on the Brahman only after the Brahman is known.[72]

These statements are then followed by the comment: "As the ancient advaitins accepted the authority of the Śruti, and took the truth of the Brahman for granted, they could weave out theories as to how the *jīva*s and the world can come out of the Brahman. We shall later on discuss whether such attempts are useful or futile."[73]

The reference to the analogy of the dream-marks it out the first as the most promising of the three — the one which might approximate closest to Ramaṇa's position. This is confirmed by the fact that according to Ramaṇa "the *vāsanā*s must be with one's self and can never remain away from the self."[74] Indeed "the self is in the heart and the *vāsanā*s are also there in an exceedingly subtle form."[75] All else follows from the *vāsanās*.[76] As for the criticism "How the *jīva*, who is the

---

72. *Ibid.*
73. *Ibid.*
74. *Talks with Śrī Ramaṇa Maharṣi*, p. 577.
75. *Ibid.*
76. A careful statement of this is found in Paul Brunton and Munagala Venkataramiah, *op. cit.*, pp. 65-66. Therein the following two statements are found in succession: "The world is the result of the ego. Find out the ego. Its source is the final goal" (*ibid.*, pp. 65-66). This is followed by: "The world is a result of your mind. Know your mind" (*ibid.*, p. 66) However, we are also told that the "mind" arises *after* the I-thought (*ibid.*, p. 108) and subsequently even more explicitly: "The sense of the body is a thought; the thought is of the mind, the mind arises from the I-thought; the I-thought is the root-thought" (*ibid.*). Later on we are told: "The Universe is on account of the I-thought" (*ibid.*, p. 109). This fine point seems to distinguish Ramaṇa's theory from the usual version.

product of *avidyā*, can create *avidyā* through his cognitive act,"[77] Ramaṇa's following remarks on *yugapat sṛṣṭi* seem to shed some light on the matter.[78]

The point regarding *yugapat* needs to be especially noted. The doctrine wishes to avoid the pitfall of prioritization involved in regarding one as the effect or cause of another. The difficulties of the kind posited by Raju arise "only if we regard the one as preceding the other. But if we regard ignorance and individuality as but the two interdependent aspects of the same fact, as a circle and its circumference, or a triangle and its sides, or fatherhood and sonship, the difficulty does not arise."[79]

The point of the matter is that Ramaṇa's etiology is to be distinguished from his soteriology. Whereas he promotes simultaneously the *emergence* of subject and object in the process of creation, he promotes the *submergence* of the object in the subject, and moreover in one subject as part of his soteriology. The failure to recognize this has caused much confusion:

> Three persons came on a short visit; the eldest of them asked: There is one process of creation mentioned in the Upaniṣads and another in Purāṇas. Which of them is true?
>
> M.: They are many, and meant to indicate that the creation has a cause, and a creator should be posited so that one might seek the cause. The emphasis is on the purpose of the theory and not on the process of creation. Moreover, the creation is perceived by some one. There are no objects without the subject, i.e., the objects do not come and tell you

---

77. P.T. Raju, *op. cit.*, p. 103.

78. *Talks with Śrī Ramaṇa Maharṣi*, pp. 612-13.

79. Satischandra Chatterjee and Dhirendramohan Datta, *An Introduction to Indian Philosophy*, Calcutta (Kolkata): University of Calcutta, 1950, p. 421.

that they are, but it is you who say that there are the objects. The objects are therefore what the seer makes of them. They have no existence independent of the subject. Find out what you are and then you understand what the world is. That is the object of the theory.

D.: The soul is only a small particle whereas the creation is so huge. How can we surmises it?

M.: The particle speaks of the huge creation; where is the contradiction?[80]

Once this point is clearly understood the issue seems to become more tractable. For instance, examples which on the face of it seem to imply *eka-jīva-vāda* turn out really to be participating in this trend towards the unification of the subject, especially on the metaphor of the world as dream:

Only waking up from sleep, the man perceives the body and the world, but not in sleep. On the strength of the present he understands that he remained in deep sleep also. Therefore in sleep *jīva* must be concluded to be in pure state in which the body and the world are not perceived.

D.: Is not *jīva* the reflected light, the "I" — thought?

M.: He is also a *jīva*; before it also he is *jīva*; the one of them is related to the other as cause and effect. The sleeper *jīva* cannot be independent of *Īśvara*.[81]

Even though Ramaṇa's parting shot on this and the preceding discussion is — "All these are only polemics"[82] — some points are worth pursuing, especially the *jīva-Īśvara* relationship in the light of the earlier discussions. Again, in elaborating the *prātibhāsika* view, which he seems to favour as a whole, he

80. *Talks with Śrī Ramaṇa Maharṣi*, pp. 353-54.

81. *Ibid.*, p. 535.

82. *Ibid.*, p. 536.

says: "The *jagat, jīva,* and *Īśvara* are all cognised by the seer only. They do not have an existence independent of him. So there is only one *jīva,* be it the individual or God. All else is simply a myth."[83] This only makes sense as a transitional passage to the following:

> A question was asked why it was wrong to say that there is a multiplicity of *jīva*s. *Jīva*s are certainly many. For a *jīva* is only the ego and forms the reflected light of the Self. Multiplicity of selves may be wrong but not of *jīva*s.
>
> M.: *Jīva* is called so because he sees the world. A dreamer sees many *jīva*s in a dream but all of them are not real. The dreamer alone exists and he sees all. So it is with the individual and the world. There is the creed of only one Self which is also called the creed of only one *jīva*. It says that the *jīva* is only one who sees the whole world and the *jīva* is only one who sees the whole world and the *jīva*s therein.
>
> D.: Then *jīva* means the Self here.
>
> M.: So it is. But the Self is not a seer. But here he is said to see the world. So he is differentiated as the *jīva*.[84]

This comes as close to the *eka-jīva-vāda* theory as one possibly can, *except* that elsewhere that view is strenuously denied[85] or avoided![86] Ramaṇa says in no uncertain terms: "*It is only the individual mind that sees the world,*"[87] a point he makes to Major A.W. Chadwick and confirms as follows in his conversation with Paul Brunton.

> D.: Did not Mr. Brunton find you in London? Was it only a dream?

83. *Ibid.*, pp. 373-74.
84. *Ibid.*, pp. 530-31.
85. *Ibid.*, p. 518.
86. David Godman, ed., *op. cit.*, p. 189.
87. *Talks with Śrī Ramaṇa Maharṣi*, p. 518, emphasis added.

M.: Yes. He had the vision. He saw me in his mind.

D.: Did he not see this concrete form?

M.: Yes, still in his mind.[88]

This enables the issue of the problem of "the impossibility of communication between *jīvas*" to be tackled afresh. It is as if we can also shake hands with the other person, but with gloves on. We interact with other *jīvas* but through the mental film.

There are several variations of the theme of the dream-metaphor found in Ramaṇa, revealing different dimensions of his view of the world as dream. For instance, Ramaṇa found no conflict between practising *dhyāna* and pursuing one's duties: "As you practise *dhyāna* you develop your powers and you will be able to attend to both. You will begin to *look on business as a dream*."[89] When asked to reconcile Janaka's being a *jñānī* with his also functioning as a king he remarked: "Perhaps it is like a dream, just as we speak of our dreams, so they [the *jñānī*s] think of their actions."[90] Ramaṇa reported: "It is said that awakening from ignorance is like awakening from a fearful dream of a beast"[91] and used the dream-metaphor elsewhere more elaborately to explain Realization:

> The realised sage finally declares that in the regenerate state the *jāgrat* world also is found to be as unreal as the *dream* world is found to be in the *jāgrat* state.[92]

Such a view of the universe will have its own views of the *jīva*'s movement through life, death, and incarnation and of heaven and hell. According to the metaphor of the world as

88. *Ibid*. p. 207.
89. *Ibid*., p. 37.
90. *Ibid*., p. 136.
91. *Ibid*., p. 590.
92. *Ibid*., p. 372.

dream, just as places we see in dreams come to us, we don't go to them, so is it in life:

> Lying down on your bed in a closed room with eyes closed you *dream* of London, the crowds there and you among them. A certain body is identified as yourself in the dream. London and the rest could not have entered into the room and into your brain; however, such wide space and duration of time were all perceptible to you. They must have been projected from the brain. Although the world is so big and the brain so small, it is not a matter of wonder that such a big creation is contained in such a small compass as one's brain? Though the *screen* is limited, still all the pictures of the cinema pass on it and are visible there. You do not wonder how such a long procession of events could be manifest on such a small screen. Similarly with the objects and the brain.[93]

At the moment of death too "while gasping the person is in something like a dream, not aware of his present environment"[94] — sort of dream in a dream, one might say. As for reincarnation. "What happens in a dream? Do you go to the dream or does it occur to you? Surely the latter. Just the same with incarnations. The ego remains changeless all along:"[95]

Questions about heaven and hell were also raised with Ramaṇa.

> D.: Are there heaven (*swarga*) and hell (*naraka*)?
>
> M.: There must be *someone* to go there. They are like dreams. We see time and space exist in dream also.[96]

---

93. *Ibid.*, p. 148.
94. *Ibid.*, p. 201.
95. *Ibid.*, p. 271.
96. *Ibid.*, p. 45.

Even more pointedly it is clarified that "You carry heaven and hell with you. Your lust, anger, etc. produce these regions. They are like dreams"[97] — an approach reminiscent of Zen.

> A soldier named Nobushige came to Hakuin, and asked: Is there really a paradise and a hell?
>
> "Who are you?" inquired Hakuin.
>
> "I am a samurai," the warrior replied.
>
> "You, a soldier!" exclaimed Hakuin. "What kind of ruler would have you as his guard? Your face looks like that of a beggar."
>
> Nobushige became so angry that he began to draw his sword, but Hakuin continued: "So you have a sword! Your weapon is probably much too dull to cut off my head."
>
> As Nobushige drew his sword Hakuin remarked: "Here open the gates of hell!"
>
> At these words the samurai, perceiving the master's discipline, sheathed his sword and bowed.
>
> "Here open the gates of paradise," said Hakuin.[98]

Even the experience of God is cast in the dream metaphor at times by Ramaṇa:

> Yes. God is seen in the mind. The concrete form may be seen. Still it is only in the devoted mind. The form and appearance of God-manifestation are determined by the mind of the devotee. But it is not the finality. Here is the sense of duality.
>
> It is like a *dream*-vision. After God is perceived, *vicāra* commences. That ends in Realization of the Self. *Vicāra* is the ultimate route.

---

97. *Ibid.*, p. 46.

98. Paul Reps, compiler, *Zen Flesh, Zen Bones,* New York: Doubleday & Company, Inc., 1961, pp. 51-52. The next quotation is from p. 207 of *Talks with Śrī Ramaṇa Maharṣi.*

> Of course, a few find *vicāra* practicable. Others find *bhakti* easier.

The question of harmonization of the world as we know it, with the world as a dream, naturally bothered many who questioned Ramaṇa though it did not seem to bother him. He had clearly declared: "the so-called waking state is itself an illusion."[99] But he was pressed much on this point as it flies in the face of normal experience so flagrantly. A host of issues surface in the following dialogue of 3rd May, 1938:

> The same lady continued:
>
> If the world is only a *dream*, how should it be harmonized with the Eternal Reality?
>
> M.: The harmony consists in the realization of its inseparateness from the Self.
>
> D.: But a dream is fleeting and unreal. It is also contradicted by the waking state.
>
> M.: The waking experiences are similar.
>
> D.: One lives fifty years and finds a continuity in the waking experience which is absent in dreams.
>
> M.: You go to sleep and dream a dream in which the experiences of fifty years are condensed within the short duration of the dreams, say five minutes. There is also a continuity in the dream. Which is real now? Is the period covering fifty years of your waking state real or the short duration of the five minutes of your dream? The standards of time differ in the two states. That is all. There is no other difference between the experiences.
>
> D.: The spirit remains unaffected by the passing phenomena and by the successive bodies of repeated births. How does each body get the life to set it acting?

---

99. *Ibid.*, p. 166.

M.: The spirit is differentiated from matter and is full of life. The body is animated by it.

D.: The realised being is then the spirit and unaware of the world.

M.: He sees the world but not as separate from the Self.

D.: If the world is full of pain why should he continue the world-idea?

M.: Does the realised being tell you that the world is full of pain? It is the other one who feels pain and seeks the help of the wise saying that the world is painful. Then the wise one explains from his experience that if one withdraws within the Self there is an end of pain. The pain is felt so long as the object is different from oneself. But when the Self is found to be an undivided whole who and what is there to feel? The realised mind is the Holy Spirit and the other mind is the home of the devil. For the realised being this is the Kingdom of Heaven. "The Kingdom of Heaven is within you. That kingdom is here and now."[100]

This harmonization was attempted in a large number of issues, including those of science. Two outstanding examples of the latter are Ramaṇa's views on evolution and the mind-brain relationship. Ramaṇa regarded evolution as a post-facto rationalization of a given state of affairs, as when, on seeing an old building in a dream *momentarily*, we may *wrongly* deduce that thousands of years must have elapsed since its construction! Ramaṇa gives a similar if less sensational account elsewhere: "One sees an edifice in his *dream*. It rises up all of a sudden. Then he begins to think how it should have been already built brick by brick by so many labourers during such a long time. Yet he does not see the builders working. So also with the theory of evolution. Because he finds himself a man

100. *Ibid.*, p. 469

he thinks that he has developed to that stage from the primal state of the amoeba."[101] His views on brain-mind may interest psychologists, just as his views on evolution might interest biologists:

> Further conversations led to the question if the mind was identical with the brain. Śrī Bhagavān said: The mind is only a force operating on the brain. You are now here and awake. The thoughts of the world and the surroundings are in the *brain* within the body. When you *dream* you create another self who sees the world of dream creation and the surroundings just as you do now. The dream visions are in the *dream* brain which is again in the dream body. That is different from your present body. You remember the dream now. The brains are however different. Yet the visions appear in the mind. The mind therefore is not identical with the brain. Waking, dream and sleep are for the mind only.[102]

And at the opposite end of the spectrum from the scientific, the miraculous too was sought to be harmonised: "How can there be miracles at all? If they are said to surpass human understanding so are creations in dreams."[103]

But from a spiritual point of view the most significant harmonization had to be between the divergent outlooks of the man of the world and the man in it but not of it — the *ajñānī* and the *jñānī*. Ramaṇa identifies the problem first and then illustrates it with the analogy of a dream.

> An *ajñānī* sees someone as a *jñānī* and identifies him with the body. Because he does not know the Self and mistakes his body for the Self, he extends the same mistake to the

---

101. *Ibid.*, p. 603.
102. *Ibid.*, pp. 455-56.
103. *Ibid.*, p. 443.

> state of the *jñānī*. The *jñānī* is therefore considered to be the physical frame.
>
> Again since the *ajñānī*, though he is not the doer, yet imagines himself to be the doer and the actions of the body his own, he thinks the *jñānī* to be similarly acting when the body is active. But the *jñānī* himself knows the Truth and is not confounded. The state of a *jñānī* cannot be determined by the *ajñānī* and therefore the question troubles only the *ajñānī* and never does it arise for the *jñānī*. If he is a doer he must determine the nature of the actions. The Self cannot be the doer. Find out who is the doer and the Self is revealed.[104]

When, however, he was told: "So it amounts to this. To see a *jñānī* is not to understand him. You see the jñānī's body and not his *jñānam*. One must therefore be a *jñānī* to know a *jñānī*."[105] He remarked:

> M.: The *jñānī* sees no one as *ajñānī*. All are only *jñānī*s in his sight. In the ignorant state one superimposes his ignorance on a *jñānī* and mistakes him for a doer. In the state of *jñāna*, the *jñānī* sees nothing separate from the Self. The Self is all shining and only pure *jñāna*. So there is no *ajñāna* in his sight. There is an illustration for this kind of illusion or superimposition. Two friends went to sleep side by side. One of them *dreamt* that both of them had gone on a long journey and had strange experiences. On waking up he recapitulated them and asked his friend if it was not so. The other one simply ridiculed him saying that it was only his dream and could not affect the other.
>
> So it is with the *ajñānī* who superimposes his illusive ideas on others.

---

104. *Ibid.*, p. 479
105. *Ibid.* The following citation is from p. 480.

5

The Use of the Dream-Metaphor in Advaita Vedānta: Nisargadatta Mahārāja

THE use of the dream-metaphor by Ramaṇa and Nisargadatta is so common and similar that it borders on the astounding. As Ramaṇa has already been invoked often, we would refer more frequently to Nisargadatta in what follows in the interest of impartiality. Nisargadatta clearly advises his interlocutor to treat life as a dream: "the world you can perceive is a very small world indeed. And it is entirely private. Take it to be a dream and be done with it"[1] was his exhortation.

He elaborated his position as follows:

> Or, take another example. We wake and we sleep. After a day's work sleep comes. Now, do I go to sleep or does inadvertence — characteristic of the sleeping state — come to me? In other words — we are awake because we are asleep. We do not wake up into a really waking state. In the waking state the world emerges due to ignorance and takes one into a waking-dream state. Both sleep and waking are misnomers. We are only dreaming. True waking and true sleeping *only the jñānī knows*. We dream that we are awake, we dream that we are asleep. The three states are only varieties of the dream state. *Treating everything as a dream liberates*. As long as you give reality to dreams, you are their

1. Maurice Frydman, tr., *op. cit.*, p. 23.

> slave. By imagining that you are born as so-and-so, you become a slave to the so-and-so. The essence of slavery is to imagine yourself to be a process, to have past and future, to have history. In fact, we have no history, we are not a process, we do not develop, nor decay; also see all as a dream and stay out of it.[2]

One way to wake up from this dream is to "create so much trouble for yourself that you have to wake up." There is no assumption here that one wakes up only through suffering; "enquiry also wakes you up."[3] When challenged why he was doing nothing to wake up the interlocutor, he responded:

> M.: I am doing: I did enter your dreamlike state to tell you — "Stop hurting yourself and others, stop suffering, wake up."
>
> Q.: Why then don't we wake up?
>
> M.: You will. I shall not be thwarted. It may take some time. When you shall begin to question your dream, awakening will be not far away.[4]

The same theme crops up again.

> Q.: Still, there is duality, there is sorrow, there is need of help. By denouncing it as mere dream nothing is achieved.
>
> M.: The only thing that can help is to wake up from the dream.
>
> Q.: An awakener is needed.
>
> M.: Who again is in the dream. The awakener signifies the beginning of the end. There are no eternal dreams.
>
> Q.: Even when it is beginningless?
>
> M.: Everything begins with you. What else is beginningless?

---

2. *Ibid*. p. 189.
3. *Ibid*., p. 68. This can impart a whole new dimension to the understanding of *Brahma-Sūtra* 1.1.1!
4. *Ibid*., pp. 73-74.

Q.: I began at birth.

M.: That is what you are told. Is it so? Did you see yourself beginning?

Q.: I began just now. All else is memory.

M.: Quite right. The beginningless begins forever . . .[5]

When the dream-metaphor was pushed to the point of recognizing Nisargadatta too as a dream, though as a "most unusual dream" he responded: "I am the dream that can wake you up. You will have the proof of it in your very waking up."[6] Some of the visitors of Ramaṇa refused to accept that they were not fully awake as they were, such as the Christian missionary, Dr. Stanley Jones. The following segment of their dialogue illustrates this point:

D.: But I want to be wide awake.

M.: Is this your wide awakened state? It is not. It is only a *dream* in your long sleep. All are in sleep, dreaming of the world and things and actions.

D.: This is all Vedāntic, I have no use for it. The existing differences are not imaginary. They are positive. However, what is that real waking? Can Maharṣi tell us what he has found it to be?

M. Real waking lies beyond the three states of waking, dream and sleep.

D.: I am really awake and know that I am not in sleep.

M.: Real waking lies beyond the plane of differences.

D.: What is the state of the world then?

M.: Does the world come and tell you "I exist"?

D= Devotee, M= Maharṣi.

5. *Ibid.*, pp. 106-107.

6. *Ibid.*, p. 181.

D.: No. But the people in the world tell me that the world needs spiritual, social and moral regeneration.

M.: You see the world and the people in it. They are your thoughts. Can the world be apart from you?

D.: I enter into it with love.

M.: Before entering thus do you stand aloof?

D.: I am identified with it and yet remaining apart. Now I came here to ask Maharṣi and hear him. Why does he ask me questions?

M.: Maharṣi has replied. His reply amounts to this: Real waking does not involve differences.

D.: Can such realisation be universalised?

M.: Where are differences there? There are no individuals in it.

D. Have you reached the goal?

M.: The goal cannot be anything apart from the Self: nor can it be something to be gained afresh. If that were so, such goal cannot be abiding and permanent. What appears anew will also disappear. The goal must be eternal and within. Find it within yourself.

D.: I want to know your experience.

M.: Maharṣi does not seek enlightenment. The question is of no use to the questioner. Whether I have realised or not, how does it affect the questioner?

D.: Not so. Each one's experience has a human value in it and can be shared by others.

M.: The problem must be solved by the questioner himself. The question is best directed to oneself.[7]

Ramaṇa had this to say for those who recognized the need to wake up from the dream: "That sleep which alternates with

7. *Talks with Śrī Ramaṇa Maharṣi*, pp. 453-54.

waking is not true sleep. That waking which alternates with sleep is not true waking. Are you now awake? You are not. You are required to wake up to your real state. You should not fall into false sleep nor keep falsely awake."[8] However while "falsely awake," that is, while in the waking state one can work towards and attain Self-Realization: "The incentive to realise can arise only in the waking state and effort can be made only when one is awake,"[9] leading to *atijāgrat* beyond wakefulness,"[10] that is, to Realization.

The preceding account does render the possibility plausible that *mokṣa* may be attained from within *māyā* through *māyā*. But why seek *mokṣa*? Ramaṇa's response to this could be curt: "Why should you seek Self-Realization? Why do you not rest content with your present situation . . ."[11]

Nisargadatta is more forthcoming and elaborates the point with the help of the dream-metaphor:

> Q.: The Supreme Reality (Parabrahman) may be present in all of us. But of what use is it to us?
>
> M.: You are like a man who says: "I need a place where to keep my things, but of what use is space to me?" or "I need milk, tea, coffee or soda, but for water I have no use." Don't you see that the Supreme Reality is what makes everything possible? But if you ask of what use is it to you, I must answer: "None." In matters of daily life the knower of the real has no advantage: he may be at a disadvantage rather: being free from greed and fear, he does not protect himself. The very idea of profit is foreign to him; he abhors accretions; his life is constant divesting oneself, giving.

---

8. *Talks with Śrī Ramaṇa Maharṣi*, p. 476.
9. *Ibid.*, p. 563.
10. *Ibid.*, p. 564.
11. *Ibid.*, 466.

Q.: If there is no advantage in gaining the Supreme, then why take the trouble?

M.: There is trouble only when you cling to something. When you hold on to nothing, no trouble arises. The relinquishing of the lesser is the gaining of the greater. Give up all and you gain all. Then life becomes what it was meant to be: pure radiation from an inexhaustible source. In that light the world appears dimly like a dream.

Q.: If my world is merely a dream and you are a part of it, what can you do for me? If the dream is not real, having no being, how can reality affect it?

Q.: You seem to take for granted that there can be a dream without a dreamer and that I identify myself with the dream of my own sweet will. But I am the dreamer and the dream too. Who is to stop dreaming?

M.: Let the dream unroll itself to its very end. You cannot help it. But you can look at the dream as a dream, refuse it the stamp of reality.

Q.: Here am I, sitting before you. I am dreaming and you are watching me talking in my dream. What is the link between us?

M.: My intention to wake you up is the link. My heart wants you awake. I see you suffer in your dream and I know that you must wake up to end your woes. When you see your dream as dream, you wake up. But in your dream itself I am not interested. Enough for me to know that you must wake up. You need not bring your dream to a definite conclusion, or make it noble, or happy, or beautiful; all you need is to realise that you are dreaming. Stop imagining, stop believing. See the contradictions, the incongruities, the falsehood and the sorrow of the human state, the need to go beyond. Within the immensity of space floats a tiny atom of consciousness and in it the entire universe is contained.

Q.: There are affections in the dream which seem real and everlasting. Do they disappear on waking up?

> M.: In dream you love some and not others. On waking up you find you are love itself, embracing all. Personal love, however intense and genuine, invariably binds; love in freedom is love of all.
>
> Q.: People come and go. One loves whom one meets, one cannot love all.
>
> M.: When you are love itself, you are beyond time and numbers. In loving one you love all, in loving all, you love each. One and all are not exclusive.
>
> Q.: You say you are in a timeless state. Does it mean that past and future are open to you? Did you meet Vaṣiṣṭa Muni, Rāma's Guru?
>
> M.: The question is in time and about time. Again you are asking me about the contents of a dream. Timelessness is behond the illusion of time, it is not an extension in time. He who called himself Vaṣiṣṭa knew Vaṣiṣṭa. I am beyond all names and shapes. Vaṣiṣṭa is a dream in your dream. How can I know him? You are too much concerned with past and future. It is all due to your longing to continue, to protect yourself against extinction. And as you want to continue, you want others to keep you company, hence your concern with their survival. But what you call survival is but the survival of a dream. Death is preferable to it. There is a chance of waking up.[12]

Sometimes his co-locutors got fed up with Nisargadatta's use of the dream-metaphor, the way the antagonists of Śaṅkara had got fed up with his use of *māyā*, and exclaimed: "Your assumption that we are in a dream state makes your position unassailable"[13] but more often they were curious about where he was coming from, so to say. And sometimes he would fall back on that sturdy standby, the dream-metaphor:

---

12. Maurice Frydman, tr., *op. cit.*, pp. 257-59.
13. *Ibid.*, p. 368.

Q.: Please tell us more.

M.: Talking is not my hobby. Sometimes I talk, sometimes I do not. My talking, or not talking, is a part of a given situation and does not depend on me. When there is a situation in which I have to talk, I hear myself talking. It is all the same to me. Whether I talk or not, the light and love of being what I am are not affected, nor are they under my control. They are, and I know they are. There is a glad awareness, but nobody who is glad. Of course, there is sense of identity, but it is the identity of a memory trace, like the identity of a sequence of pictures on the ever-present screen. Without the light and the screen there can be no picture. To know the picture as the play of light on the screen, gives freedom from the idea that the picture is real. All you have to do is to understand that you love the self and the self loves you, and that the sense "I am" is the link between you both, a token of identity in spite of apparent diversity. Look at the "I am" as a sign of love between the inner and the outer, the real and the appearance. *Just like in a dream all are different, except the sense of "I" which enables you to say "I dreamt," so does the sense of "I am" enable you to say "I am my real Self" again. I do nothing, or is anything done to me.* I am what I am and nothing can affect me. I appear to depend on everything, but in fact all depend on me.[14]

The dream-metaphor is thus continually and consistently employed by Ramaṇa and Nisargadatta. Often the statement by one of them is imperceptibly transformed, as it were, into the dream-metaphor of another — undergoing not merely metamorphosis but metaphor-morphosis if you like. Ramaṇa, for instance, while describing the vision of God almost imperceptibly adds the remark: "It is like a dream-vision."

---

14. *Ibid.*, p. 388, emphasis added.

When asked if Paul Brunton saw him in a dream in London, Ramaṇa said: "Yes. He had a vision."[15]

In Nisargadatta's case the same point emerges in the following guise:

> Q.: If I am light only how did I come to forget it?
>
> M.: You have not forgotten. It is in the picture on the screen that you forget and then remember. You never cease to be a man because you dream to be a tiger. Similarly you are pure light appearing as a picture on the screen and also becoming one with it.
>
> Q.: Since all happens, why should I worry?
>
> M.: Exactly. Freedom is freedom from worry. Having realised that you cannot influence the results, pay no attention to your desires and fears. Let them come and go. Don't give them the nourishment of interest and attention.
>
> Q.: If I turn my attention from what happens, what am I to live by?
>
> M.: Again it is like asking: "What shall I do, if I stop dreaming?" Stop and see. You need not be anxious: "What next?" There is always the next.[16]

Ramaṇa describes the predicament of Advaitic pedagogy with a spatial metaphor.

> There are different ways to Tiruvannāmalai, but Tiruvannāmalai is the same by whichever way it is gained. Similarly the approach to Realization varies according to the personality. Yet the Self is the same. *But still, being in Tiruvannāmalai, to ask the way to it is ridiculous. So also, being the Self, to ask how to realise the Self looks absurd.* You are the Self. Remain as the Self. That is all. Questions arise because

---

15. *Talks with Śrī Ramaṇa Maharṣi*, p. 207.

16. Maurice Frydman, tr., *op. cit.*, p. 481.

> of the present wrong identification of the Self with the body. That is ignorance. That must go. On its removal the Self alone is.[17]

He also adds:

> There is no greater mystery than this, that being the Reality ourselves, we seek to gain Reality. We think that there is something binding our Reality and that it must be destroyed before the Reality is gained. It is ridiculous. A day will dawn when we will ourselves laugh at our efforts. That which is on the day of laughter is also now.
>
> The very doubt "Can I realise?" or the feeling "I have not realised," are obstacles to Realization. Realization is not something to be gained afresh. The Self is already realised. All that is necessary is to get rid of the thought "I have not realised."[18]

Nisargadatta presses the dream metaphor into service in a similar context. Once, when asked about the Real, push came to shove and he was interrogated sharply: "does it exist, or is it a concept only, a verbal opposition to the changeable?" He replied:

> M.: It is, it alone is. But in your present state it is of no use to you. Just like the glass of water near your bed is of no use to you, when you dream that you are dying of thirst in a desert. I am trying to wake you up, whatever your dream.
>
> Q.: Please don't tell me that I am dreaming and that I will soon wake up. I wish it were so. But I am awake and in pain. You talk of a painless state, but you add that I cannot have it in my present condition. I feel lost.
>
> M.: Don't feel lost. I only say that to find the immutable and blissful you must give up your hold on the mutable and

---

17. Swami Rajeswarananda, compiler, *op. cit.*, pp. 15-16, emphasis added.

18. *Ibid.*, p. 49.

> painful. You are concerned with your own happiness and I am telling you that there is no such thing. Happiness is never your own, it is where the "I" is not. I do not say it is beyond your reach; you have only to reach out beyond yourself, and you will find it.[19]

Ramaṇa says: "He who is forgetful of the Self, mistaking the physical body for it, and goes through innumerable births, is like one who wanders all over the world in a dream."[20] Nisargadatta must have said as much to his co-locutor who burst out:

> Q.: You keep on telling me that I am dreaming and that it is high time I should wake up. How does it happen that the Mahārāj, who has come to me in my dreams, has not succeeded in waking me up? He keeps on urging and reminding, but the dream continues.
>
> M.: It is because you have not really understood that you are dreaming. This is the essence of bondage — the mixing of the real with unreal. In your present state only the sense "I am" refers to reality; the "what" and the "how I am" are illusions imposed by destiny or accident.
>
> Q.: When did the dream begin?
>
> M.: It appears to be beginningless, but in fact it is only now. From moment to moment you are renewing it. Once you have seen that you are dreaming, you shall wake up. But you do not see, because you want the dream to continue. A day will come when you will long for the ending of the dream, with all your heart and mind, and be willing to pay any price; the price will be dispassion and detachment, the loss of interest in the dream itself.

---

19. Maurice Frydman, tr., *op.cit.*, p. 439.
20. Swami Rajeswarananda, compiler, *op. cit.*, pp. 13-14.

> Q.: How helpless I am. As long as the dream of existence lasts, I want it to continue. As long as I want it to continue, it will last.
>
> M.: Wanting it to continue is not inevitable. See clearly your condition, your very clarity will release you.[21]

The Advaitic convergences between Ramaṇa and Nisargadatta keep surfacing through their statements. "I exist" says Ramaṇa, "is the only permanent, self-evident experience of every one. Nothing is so self-evident (*pratyakṣa*) as "I am."[22] When Nisargadatta was asked what causes such beingness to arise, he replied: "Just as you have no cause for your dream, there is no cause for the beingness. Explain to me how you have a dream. It is causeless; therefore it is without logic."[23] How the universe arose out of I-Amness is also explained by Nisargadatta with the help of the dream-metaphor. "In the process, when you go to the source itself, you will realise that "I Amness" contains this manifested universe, like a seed. To understand more clearly take the example of the dream-world. You are in deep sleep and suddenly you feel "I am," and that "I Amness" creates a dream world. Similarly this manifest world is created by that "I Amness." You will realise this later in the search for the truth. The last progress will be for you to transcend this "I Amness" also and get stabilized in the Ultimate."[24] The relationship between the beingness and the world is again explained by Nisargadatta in terms of the dream-metaphor, as he sets out to address a group of villagers:

---

21. Maurice Frydman, tr., *op. cit.*, p. 506.
22. Swami Rajeswarananda, compiler, *op. cit.*, p. 24.
23. Jean Dunn, ed., *Seeds of Consciousness: The Wisdom of Śrī Nisargadatta Mahārāj*, New York: Grove Press Inc., 1982, p. 182.
24. *Ibid.*, pp. 54-55.

> At the command of my Guru I am doing these *bhajans* and talks. When I go to that village, I shall have to talk about God and the devotee. They will not be able to understand, so I will talk at their level. For the ignorant this is all right: God is eternal, there is sin and virtue. For the ignorant all these things are true, but they are all hearsay.
>
> It is said that God and the world are ancient, eternal. When I was not I did not know about this eternal world and God. When I was not they did not exist.
>
> Take the example of the dream world. In the dream world I see a great spectacle of old castles, ancient monuments, but my dream is very fresh and new. I have the dream of the moment only, so how can the spectacle be ancient? Similarly, this also is for the moment. So long as the beingness is there the world is there. Without my beingness there is no world.
>
> I believe that you are listening to my talks and understanding properly. If that be so, why should you have any fear of death? Finally, what is death? This body is like a lamp with fuel, and the wick is aflame with beingness. You know that when the fuel is exhausted the flame will disappear, the "I Amness" will disappear.
>
> My Guru told me to be one with that beingness, and when you are one with it, that very principle will disclose to you all the mysteries of this beingness and in that process you will transcend it; but be very humble, be very devoted.[25]

Unlike Nisargadatta, Ramaṇa never went out to preach.[26] Perhaps each had their own dream-worlds to live in and live by! Their paralleling of living with dreaming is so striking that another example may be cited. The context is provided by a discussion of the post-mortem state.

---

25. *Ibid.*, pp. 199-200.
26. Arthur Osborne, *Ramaṇa Maharṣi and the Path of Self-Knowledge*, York Beach, Maine: Samuel Weiser, Inc., 1995, Chapter VI.

> Q.: There seems to be a lot of evidence that consciousness does somehow continue after death.
>
> M.: It is a concept. Actually no one has an experience even of the birth and death of this life.
>
> Q.: How did they happen?
>
> M.: Have you had any dreams?
>
> Q.: Yes.
>
> M.: You are also present in your own dreams and you see yourself as someone totally different; at the end of the dream it all disappears.
>
> Q.: Why did I get into this body consciousness?
>
> M.: You are sleeping safe and sound in your bed, warm and comfortable. So why do you convey yourself in dreams to a state where you are struggling for breath and dying in a nightmare? All this manifest is only a dream of the Unmanifest and is not really happening.
>
> That which makes us believe that we are is the cause, and at the end of it we are back in our original state. One who knows this has no fear of anything that is happening.[27]

It would seem like stretching the elasticity of the metaphor to the breaking point and even beyond, but not only is life explained in terms of the dream-metaphor, so is the person en route to Realization and the Realised being as well! The situation of the aspirant is metaphorically presented as follows:

> Q.: From what is being said it appears that all of this remains a play in consciousness and if one chooses to identify with consciousness one can play an infinite number of games.
>
> M.: Whatever one chooses or likes, he is invited to follow that profession or entertainment.

---

27. Jean Dunn, *op. cit.*, pp. 179-80.

Q.: What we have been doing is trying to find the real game to play and yet it all remains a game in consciousness.

M.: You are not playing, you are witnessing.

Q.: I have seen that what has kept me playing in consciousness is a fear that nothing will happen. The moments that I have been apparently free from consciousness, things happen anyhow, but they don't arise our of my desire. They happen because the universe pushes them.

M.: When you see that, are you in the consciousness?

Q.: At least it appears that I am out of it; I see the dream for a dream.

M.: You don't know whether you are in it or out of it; you simply witness it.

Q.: As long as there is the connection with the body it seems to me that the witness is still in the dream in some way.

M.: Yes, he is not awake, it's a dream.

Q.: It's like those moments between dream and awakening, when one is suddenly aware that one is dreaming. There is no break in the continuity of one who wakes up in that dream. I am awake in a dream.

M.: That dream is yourself. Whatever you see is not the dream, that is the "I" that you are. That consciousness that sees everything sees through the dream itself.

Q.: Will the *mantra* be useful in moments of mental fluctuation?

M.: Yes; it is for that only — to check your fluctuating mind.[28]

And when Nisargadatta was asked to describe the Realised being's perception of the universe, the dream-metaphor could not be excluded:

---

28. *Ibid.*, pp. 110-11.

> Things are happening in the world just as they used to happen, but one has realised that one has no name or form and therefore no activities. Whatever is happening in the world is in the nature of a dream. The individual personality is lost. One who knows this cannot be interested in improving such a world. He does not concern himself with the behaviour in the world.[29]

This may sound strangely callous but Ramaṇa's response was no different.

> Q.: When we suffer grief and complain and appeal to you by letter or mentally by prayer, are you not moved to feel what a pity it is that your child suffers like this?
>
> A.: If one felt like that one would not be a *jñānī*.[30]

And the reason is also explained finally through the dream-metaphor. When asked whether Realization, when gained, will help others Ramaṇa said: "Yes and it is the best help you possibly can give them." However, he then added: "But in fact there are no others to help."[31] What then of setting out to help others or of resolving to help others instead of attaining one's own Realization: "This is just like the dreamer saying: "Let all these people in the dream wake up before I do"![32]

Temptations should be resisted but it is not possible to resist this one. Do Realised beings dream? Ramana was asked:

> Q.: Does the *jñānī* have dreams?

---

29. *Ibid.*, pp. 86-87.
30. David Godman, ed., p. 211.
31. Arthur Osborne, ed., *The Teachings of Bhagavān Śrī Ramaṇa Maharṣī in His Own Words*, Tiruvannāmalai: Śrī Ramaṇasramam, 1971, p. 240.
32. *Ibid.*, p. 242. Also see, *Talks With Śrī Ramaṇa Maharṣi*, p. 478.

> A.: Yes, he does dream, but he knows it to be a dream, in the same way as he knows the waking state to be a dream. You may call them dream no. 1 and dream no. 2. The *jñānī* being established in the fourth state — *turīya*, the supreme reality — he detachedly witnesses the three other states, waking, dreaming and dreamless sleep, as pictures superimposed on it.
>
> For those who experience waking, dream and sleep, the state of wakeful sleep, which is beyond those three states, is named *turīya* [the fourth]. But since that *turīya* alone exists and since the seeming three states do not exist, know for certain that *turīya* is itself *turiyātīta* [that which transcends the fourth].[33]

In this the Hindu view differs from the Buddhist. According to Buddhists "all dream except the *arhants* who belong to the highest class and whose minds do not suffer from *viparyaya* (hallucination)."[34] This raises an interesting point: is someone who knows one is hallucinating really hallucinating?

---

33. David Godman, ed., p. 7.
34. P.T. Raju, "Indian Philosophy" in Harisdas Bhattacharyya, ed., *op. cit.*, Volume III, p. 598.

6

The World as Dream in Hindu Mythology

THE world as dream appears as an engaging theme in Hindu mythology. This vision of the world is most commonly associated with Viṣṇu, a member of the so-called Hindu trinity, whose role it is to preserve the cosmos from premature dissolution. The idea that the universe lasts so long as Viṣṇu dreams of it has its roots in the Advaitic view of God:

> When we consider the universe in reference to this supreme subject, there is only one type of reality in place of the two found in the case of the *jīva*; and that is of the phenomenal or *prātibhāsika* type. For by hypothesis whatever is, is known to *Īśvara* and no part of it lasts longer than the time during which it is experienced. In this sense, *Īśvara* may be described as an eternal dreamer. But we must not think that he is deluded. That would be so if he did not realise the identity of the objective world with himself, or if any aspect of the truth about it remained unrevealed to him. What is meant by describing *Īśvara*'s world as *prātibhāsika* is that its unity with himself being always realised, all variety as such is known to him to be a mere abstraction.[1]

Such abstraction may be represented as a dream. Moreover, being God, not only does He dream the universe, he is also aware of the dream as a dream which gives Him a kind of freedom Hindu

---

1. M. Hiriyanna, *Outlines of Indian Philosophy*, p. 367.

mythology loves to exploit. This appears clearly in the experiences of Mārkaṇḍeya. The leitmotif of these accounts is as follows. A renowned sage, Mārkaṇḍeya, is leading a pious life in our world, which is *really* a dream within Viṣṇu as he lies recumbent on his couch consisting of the primeval serpent, floating like an air-bed on the cosmic waters. On two occasions he slips out from within the body of God into the dark abyss. Our task is to provide an adequate oneric hermeneutic of these experiences.

One begins with Viṣṇu reclining on the serpent on the waters, or to embroider the theme — "It is on a serpent ocean of his own immortal substance that the Cosmic Man passes the universal night."

> Inside the god is the cosmos, like an unborn babe within the mother; and here all is restored to its primal perfection. Though without there exists only darkness, within the divine dreamer an ideal vision thrives of what the universe should be. The world, recovering from decline, confusion, and disaster, runs again the harmonious course.
>
> And now, it is during this spellbound interlude that there occurs — according to the tale — a fantastic event:
>
> A holy man, Mārkaṇḍeya by name, is wandering inside the god, over the peaceful earth, as an aimless pilgrim, regarding with pleasure the edifying sight of the ideal vision of the world. This Mārkaṇḍeya is a well-known mythical figure, a saint endowed with life unending. He is many thousands of years old, yet of unaging strength and alert mind. Wandering now through the interior of Viṣṇu's body, he is visiting the holy hermitages, gratified by the pious pursuits of the sages and their pupils. At shrines and holy places he pauses to worship, and his heart is made glad by the piety of the people in the countries through which he roams.

But now an accident occurs. In the course of his aimless, unending promenade, the sturdy man slips, inadvertently, out through the mouth of the all-containing god. Viṣṇu is sleeping with lips a little open; breathing with a deep, sonorous, rhythmical sound, in the immense silence of the night of Brahmā. And the astonished saint, falling from the sleeper's giant lip, plunges headlong into the cosmic sea.

At first, because of Viṣṇu's *māyā*, Mārkaṇḍeya does not behold the sleeping giant, but only the ocean, utterly dark, stretching far in the all-embracing, starless night. He is seized by despair, and fears for his life. Splashing about in the dark water, he becomes presently pensive, ponders, and begins to doubt. "Is it a dream? Or am I under the spell of an illusion? Forsooth, this circumstance, utterly strange, must be the product of my imagination. For the world as I know it, and as I observed it in its harmonious course, does not deserve such annihilation as it seems now suddenly to have suffered. There is no sun, no moon, no wind; the mountains have all vanished, the earth has disappeared. What manner of universe is this in which I discover myself? . . ."[2]

The saint, forlorn in the vast expanse of the waters and on the very point of despair, at last became aware of the form of the sleeping god; and he was filled with amazement and a beatific joy. Partly submerged, the enormous shape resembled a mountain range breaking out of the waters. It glowed with a wonderful light from within. The saint swam nearer, to study the presence; and he had just opened his lips to ask who this was, when the giant seized him, summarily swallowed him, and he was again in the familiar landscape of the interior.[3]

---

2. From an Advaitic point of view, this was the moment for Mārkaṇḍeya to ask: "To whom does this confusion occur?," David Godman, ed., *op. cit.*, p. 184.

3. Heinrich Zimmer, *Myths and Symbols in Indian Art and Civilization*, New York: Harper & Row, 1962; edited by Joseph Campbell, pp. 38-39, 41.

The account opens up a whole range of possible interpretations. To begin with, so long as the sage was *within* the dream, he saw the world as an ordered whole. Whether it was actually so or not is *another* issue. "All this talk about inconsistencies in the dream-world arises only. . . when you are awake. While you are dreaming, the dream-world was a perfectly integrated whole." It was "real and not illusory to you so long as you did not know that the dream itself was not illusory . . . the sensations that you have . . . get co-ordinated to give you the impression that the world is real."[4] It must also be borne in mind that the sage has not awakened from the dream. There is also in the account the lively suspense of an individual wondering whether one is dreaming or not oneself, within a cosmic dream! The next consideration is crucial. Normally one dreams at night, so that the dream can be seen as a circle of vision enclosed within an encircling darkness. This is the metaphysical reality to which the sage has been exposed — that in a sense the darkness, which constitutes the increasingly opaque boundaries of the dream as one moves away from the luminous centre, is itself in a sense a part of the scenario, just as sleeping is an integral part of dreaming — indeed a prerequisite for it! In fact, if one may be permitted a somewhat exotic reflection — if we inhabit an expanding universe and this universe be bounded as if by the thin fading orb of the light of a lamp — the more it expands the deeper are we thrown into the womb of an ever-enlarging encircling darkness. It is also worth noting that in a dream-world, in which one is a figure in a universal dream, any revelation would also seem like or possess the status of a dream!

We are now ready for the second adventure of sage Mārkaṇḍeya:

---

4. David Godman, ed., *op. cit.*, p. 189.

Mārkaṇḍeya, back again, resumed his former life. As before, he wandered over the wide earth, a saintly pilgrim. He observed yogis practising austerities in the woods. He nodded assent to the kingly donors who performed costly sacrifices, with lavish gifts for the brāhmaṇas. He watched brāhmaṇas officiating at sacrificial rituals and receiving generous fees for their effective magic. All castes he saw piously devoted to their proper tasks, and the holy sequence of the Four Stages of Life he observed in full effect among men. Graciously pleased with this ideal state of affairs, he wandered in safety for another hundred years.

But then, inadvertently, once again, he slipped from the sleeper's mouth and tumbled into the pitch-black sea. This time, in the dreadful darkness and water-desert of silence, he beheld a luminous babe, a godlike boy beneath a fig tree, peaceful in slumber. Then again, by an effect of *māyā*, Mārkaṇḍeya saw the lonely little boy cheerfully at play, undismayed amidst the vast ocean. The saint was filled with curiosity, but his eyes could not stand the dazzling splendour of the child, and so he remained at a comfortable distance, pondering as he kept himself afloat on the pitchy deep. Mārkaṇḍeya mused: "Something of this kind I seem to remember having beheld once before — long, long ago." But then his mind became aware of the fathomless depth of the shoreless ocean and was overcome with a freezing fear.

The god, in the guise of the divine child, gently addressed him. "Welcome, Mārkaṇḍeya!" The voice had the soft deep tone of the melodious thundering of an auspicious rain cloud. The god reassured him: "Welcome, Mārkaṇḍeya! Do not be afraid, my child. Do not fear. Come hither."[5]

---

5. Heinrich Zimmer, *Myths and Symbols in Indian Art and Civilization*, pp. 42-43.

A conversation ensues between the cosmically precocious child and the venerable sage who takes umbrage at being addressed in terms of domestic familiarity:

> When the saint had thus expressed his wroth, the divine child resumed his discourse, unperturbed. "Child, I am thy parent, thy father and elder, the primeval being who bestows all life. Why do you not come to me? I knew your sire well. He practised severe austerities in bygone times in order to beget a son. He gained my grace. Pleased with his perfect saintliness, I granted him a gift, and he requested that you, his son, should be endowed with inexhaustible life-strength and should never grow old. Your father knew the secret core of his existence, and you stem from that core. This is why you are now privileged to behold me, recumbent on the primal, all containing cosmic waters, and playing here as a child beneath the tree."
>
> Mārkaṇḍeya's features brightened with delight. His eyes grew wide, like opening blossoms. In humble surrender, he made as if to bow and he prayed: "Let me know the secret of your *māyā*, the secret of your apparition now as child, lying and playing in the infinite sea. Lord of the Universe, by what name are you known? I believe you to be the Great Being of all beings; for who else could exist as you exist?"

Viṣṇu replied: "I am the Primeval Cosmic Man, Nārāyaṇa."[6]

---

6. *Ibid.*, p. 44. A somewhat different account of Mārkaṇḍeya's encounter with the divine child is also found. "One evening at dusk Mārkaṇḍeya was sitting at Puṣpabhadratīra when from somewhere a wind began to blow. The wind increased in strength and the sky became covered with clouds. The place resounded with peals of thunder and soon it began to rain. Rains became heavy. Rivers became flooded and water-level in the oceans rose. Everything around was submerged in water and Mārkaṇḍeya alone stood there with his matted hair swinging in the wind. It

→

This account also sends hermeneutical sparks flying in all directions. First of all, "Find the seer and the creation is comprised in him,"[7] "Knowledge of the world is knowledge of the knower of the world."[8] These statements can be applied either to the *jīva* or to *Īśvara* in this context. But this leads to the even more alluring interpretation — that God appeared in His own cosmic dream as a child, but on the dark periphery of it rather than its luminous core. This "infantile" epiphany in darkness seems to answer, through its manner and speech, in mythological terms the metaphysical question: "What is the standard of Reality? That alone is real which exists by itself and which is eternal and unchanging."[9] Mārkaṇḍeya's mythic experiences illustrate the fact that for an ordinary mortal, be he an even pious Methasulah, "the standard of reality is the

→ was impossible to know the directions and Mārkaṇḍeya started walking. He fell into whirlpools but was the next instant thrown up on to the top of surging waves. Then he saw on the top of a high wave a banyan tree. On a branch on the north-east of the tree he saw an infant lying, devouring the darkness by its effulgence. He was attracted to the infant by its vital force and went inside the infant as it inhaled. Inside the belly of the kid Mārkaṇḍeya had a vision of the entire universe. He saw the sky, the horizon, the stars, the oceans, the mountains, expanses of land, Suras, Asuras, forests and all that the universe contained in its proper set-up. He saw passing before his eyes the elements, the Yugas and the Manvantaras. After some time he was thrown out by an exhalation of the infant. He stood on the waters. The old banyan tree was still there. An infant was still lying on a leaf on that tree. Mārkaṇḍeya then knew it was Mahāviṣṇu. He rushed to embrace the child; but the child disappeared before he reached it. Mārkaṇḍeya praised Mahāviṣṇu," Vettam Mani, *Puranic Encyclopedia*, Delhi: Motilal Banarsidass, 1975, p. 488.

7. David Godman, ed., *op. cit.*, p. 185.
8. *Ibid.*, p. 191.
9. *Ibid.*, p. 190.

waking state whereas for God, *jñāna* incarnate the standard of reality is reality itself. This reality of pure consciousness is eternal by its nature and therefore subsists equally during what you call waking, dreaming and sleep."[10] Viṣṇu is awake (for the sage), dreaming (the universe) and sleeping (on the cosmic sea) all at the same time and subsisting through each. That God appears as a child can also be endowed with a significance beyond the Wordsworthian inversion of child being the father of man. For the Realised being, existing in the world in the post-Realization phase, is often compared to a child.[11]

Moreover, the appearance of God himself in the dream in a way in which he is outside it seems like a magnification of the ordinary experience of us, being present in our dream, not as within it but as watching it from without. For it is a common experience in dreams that we can see without eyes, hear without ears, smell without nose, touch without hands and taste without tongue — that is, we may not be present within our own dreams with a dream-body and yet experience the sensations. The most identifiable of such experiences is that of sight — we may "see" a beautiful landscape in a dream without ourselves being actually physically present within the dream.

One famous depiction of the scene of Viṣṇu reclining on the serpent (independently of the stories associated with it above) is found in the Daśāvatāra Viṣṇu Temple at Deogarh, where the relief on the south wall shows Viṣṇu in the *śeṣaśāyin* or *anantaśāyin* pose, namely, reclining on the cosmic serpent. It is assigned to the sixth century CE, to the Gupta period of Indian history. Joseph Campbell has offered an interpretation

---

10. *Ibid.*, pp. 37-38.
11. *Talks With Ramaṇa Maharṣi*, pp. 3, 385-86, 572.

of this panel in terms of the world as dream which goes beyond anything found in Indological interpretations of it, or even speculation around it.[12] In the words of Campbell, the panel is a classic Hindu representation of the ultimate dreamer as Viṣṇu floating on the cosmic Milky Ocean, couched upon the coils of the abyssal serpent Ananta, the meaning of whose name is "unending." "In the foreground stand the five Pāṇḍava brothers, heroes of the epic *Mahābhārata*, with Draupadī, their wife: allegorically, she is the mind and they are the five senses. They are those whom the dream is dreaming. Eyes open, ready and willing to fight, the youths address themselves to this world of light in which we stand regarding them, where objects appear to be distinct from each other, an Aristotelian logic prevails, and A is not not-A. Behind them a dream-door has opened, however, to an inward, backward dimension where a vision emerges against darkness. Are these youths, we might ask, a dream of that luminous god, or is the god a dream of these youths?"[13]

The point raised interrogatively in the last sentence will occur again. In the meantime let us follow Campbell as he elaborates his interpretation:

> A lotus hovers above the dreaming Indian god, as though growing from his body, and seated on its corolla is Brahmā, the lord of light, apparent creator of this visible world, who with four radiant faces illuminates the quarters, giving visible shape to the figures of day as they rise from the night below. At his left (our right) is the frightening god Śiva, destroyer of illusions, riding with his goddess Pārvatī on their milk-white bull Nandī and followed by a member of his howling host, a

---

12. Arvind Sharma, "The Significance of Viṣṇu Reclining on the Serpent," *Religion* 16: pp. 101-14.

13. Joseph Campbell, *The Mythic Image*, p. 7.

> young wind god or Mārut; while at the Creator's right (our left) are the gods by whom the world-illusion is maintained: mighty Indra, the Indian counterpart of Zeus, on his four-tusked white elephant Airāvata (the rain-bearing cloud from which the god lets fly his fiery bolts), and beside him, on a peacock, the young war god, Śiva's son, who is called Kumāra, the "Chaste Youth," because wedded alone to his army.[14]

The other elements in the composition are then explained, especially the Goddess figure:

> The figure at Viṣṇu's feet in the role of the virtuous Indian wife, massaging his right leg and so stimulating his cosmic dream, is the goddess Śrī Lakṣmī, "Beauty and Good Fortune," who is known also as Padmā, "Lady Lotus." For it is actually she who had appeared symbolically in her husband's dream as the lotus wherein Brahmā thrones. There is a hymn addressed to her as the matrix of phenomenality. . . . For in dreams things are not as single, simple, and separate as they seem, the logic of Aristotle fails, and what is not-A may indeed be A. The goddess and the lotus are equivalent representations of this one life-enclosing sphere of space-time, wherein all things are brought to manifestation, multiplied, and in the end return to the universal womb that is night.[15]

As for the attendant figures, "Behind the goddess at Viṣṇu's feet stands an attendant holding the God's mace in readiness, at whose side, likewise in readiness, stands (in human form) the God's sky-carrier Garuḍa, the sun-bird on whose back he will fly to those *portions of his dream* from which cries come to him for aid . . . ."[16] Notwithstanding some issues of deviation

---

14. *Ibid.*, pp. 7-8.
15. *Ibid.*, p. 8.
16. *Ibid.*, emphasis added

from standard conceptualization and identification in the composition,[17] Joseph Campbell has succeeded in offering a persuasive interpretation of it in terms of the world as dream.

The composition can thus be broken up in these terms (1) The preserver God Viṣṇu — the *dreamer*; (2) the creator God Brahmā — above him — the *dream enhancer*; (3) the *dream-maintainers* to Brahmā's right — Indra, Airāvata and Kumāra; (4) the *dream-terminator* God (to Brahmā's left) — Śiva with his wife and pet, who saves *from* the dream; (5) the weapons, vehicle and wife of God Viṣṇu who save and serve *in* the dream; (6) the *dreamt* — the five brothers with the common wife; (7) a member of the dream dreamt symbolically within the dream — the Lady Lotus as the lotus stalk.

An intriguing aspect of the world viewed as a dream is the question: Who is dreaming whom? Is "God dreaming his creatures" — the metaphysical point of view or "is a creature dreaming his God" — a more psychological perspective. "Are the Pāṇḍavas figments of Viṣṇu's dream or is Viṣṇu a figure of theirs?"[18] Is each dreaming the other? Is there interaction between the two and of what kind? Viṣṇu is a saviour who not only preserves the dream-like cosmos from dissolution into dreamless sleep but also those within the dream, who, in distress, seek his aid. Campbell retells here the legend in the *Bhāgavata Purāṇa* VIII, 2-4[19] of Viṣṇu descending in the cosmic waters to save the earth itself in his incarnation as a boar. The macrocosmic and the microcosmic even share an oneiric resemblance. But I digress. The point Campbell makes is that Viṣṇu's vehicle, the sun bird Garuḍa is held in readiness in

17. Roy C. Craven, *A Concise History of Indian Art*, London: Thames and Hudson, 1976, p. 79.

18. Joseph Campbell, *op. cit.*, p. 10.

19. See Vettam Mani, *op. cit.*, pp. 328-29.

order that Viṣṇu may "fly to those portions of his dream from which cries come for his aid," as when he appears in the narrative of the *Bhāgavata Purāṇa* "soaring to rescue an elephant entrapped in a lotus pond by the coils of a serpent king and his spouse. (popular stories speak of a crocodile entrapping the elephant)."[20] Campbell compares the fate of the elephant to the ego-bounded personality, sinking under its own weight of self concern, as it were, in the quagmire of self-pity. For him as a dreamer, "an ego-bounded personality, interested in his own condition" is "comparable . . . to the elephant affrighted by the serpent king of a lotus pond than to the "Self" beyond selfhood reposing on the cosmic sea, through whose recollection the elephant is to be saved."[21]

This connecting cord of a common dream may involve more than a rope thrown by one dreamer to the other. In some literary passages it has been visualized as more umbilical in nature. In the controversial novel, *The Satanic Verses*, Salman Rushdie describes the relationship between the characters Mahound (Muḥammad) and Gibreel Farishta (angel Gabriel) in these terms. Thus when Mahound:

> has rested he enters a different sort of sleep, a sort of not-sleep, the condition that he calls his listening, and he feels a dragging pain in the gut, like something trying to be born, and now Gibreel, who has been hovering-above-looking-down, feels a confusion, who am I, in these moments it begins to seem that the archangel is actually inside the Prophet, I am the dragging in the gut, I am the angel being extruded from the sleeper's navel, I emerge, Gibreel Farishta, while my other self, Mahound, lies listening, entranced, I am bound to him, navel to navel, by a shining cord of light, not possible

20. Joseph Campbell, *The Mythic Image*, p. 8.
21. *Ibid*, p. 11.

> to say which of us is dreaming the other. We flow in both directions along the umbilical cord.[22]

There is also a trace of resentment that *the* Dreamer does not appear in the dream.

> Halfway into sleep, or halfway back to wakefulness, Gibreel Farishta is often filled with resentment by the non-appearance, in his persecuting visions, of the One who is supposed to have the answers, He never turns up, the one who kept away when I was dying, when I needed him. The one it's all about, Allah/Ishvar/God. Absent as ever while we writhe and suffer in his name.[23]

The question — who is in whose dream? — and the further question — is one person's dreaming (experience) another's waking (experience) — and the still further question — who is beyond all such dreaming and waking: these questions continued to tease the imagination of the Hindus and in the end produced the following tale:

> "In the country of Kosala there was once a brāhmaṇa named Gādhi. He went to the forests and standing there in water in a pond, immersed up to his neck, started doing penance. For eight months he did penance thus and then Mahāviṣṇu appeared before him and asked him what boon he wanted. The brāhmaṇa said he wanted to see *māyā-devī*. Viṣṇu granted the boon and disappeared.
>
> Several years passed after that and nothing happened. One day the brāhmaṇa as usual went to bathe in a pond. When he took a dip in the waters he forgot all his prayers and mantras. There was a change of mind. He felt he was lying

22. Salman Rushdie, *The Satanic Verses*, New York: Viking Penguin Inc., 1988, p. 110.

23. *Ibid.*, p. 111.

dead in his house. Relatives were sitting around weeping. His wife was in tears and was holding his legs. In an atmosphere of mourning, his own people weeping bitterly carried his body to a frightening burial ground and put it on a funeral pyre. It was burnt to ashes. He then felt himself in the womb of a Caṇḍāla woman living in a village near Hūṇamaṇḍala. The foetus developed and a black boy was born. The boy grew passing the stages of infancy, childhood and boyhood and became a man, black and stout. He started enjoying sexual life with a beautiful Caṇḍāla girl. The amorous plays were done on river-beds, in creeper-huts, bushes and in caves and soon many evil-natured sons were born to him. Gradually his health faded and he constructed a hermitage and lived there as a hermit. His children grew up and he became old and then all of a sudden all his children and wife and other members of his family died and he was left alone. He then left the place and travelling much reached the capital city of Kīramaṇḍala. The city gates were decorated and inside people stood in groups. The road to the palace from the gate had been beautified and as he reached the palace gates he saw an elephant as big and black as mountain standing there, well caparisoned. It was customary in those days to post an elephant well bedecked before the palace gates when a king died. The elephant he saw was the one who had been let loose to select a new king in place of the one who had just died. The elephant, on seeing him, took him by its trunk and placed him on its back. The people when they saw it shouted with joy. He was taken to the palace where he was received by young and beautiful girls. He was dressed in royal robes and he took over the administration of the state. Gradually he accepted as his wives the wives of the former King and lived there accepting the name of Gālava. He ruled the state to the satisfaction of all for eight years. One day the King went out for a stroll dressed as an ordinary man. Just outside the gate of the palace a set of Caṇḍālas were sitting singing songs to the accompaniment of a violin. As soon as they saw Gālava one of the Caṇḍālas, a red-eyed old man, got up from the group and addressing the King as "Hi, Kaluñju" shouted loudly, "Friend, where had you been all this time? It is a long time since we saw you. It is our luck we saw you at least now." The King of Kīra did not like the words of the Caṇḍāla and he rebuked the old man. The Queens and others standing on the terrace of the palace could see this scene. They were shocked. They regretted they had all along been serving a Caṇḍāla. The news spread like wild fire in the state. The King had to live in the palace without the help and co-operation of anybody inside or outside the palace.

People wanted to atone for the crime they had committed in installing a Caṇḍāla as their King. They made small fire-pits throughout the country and started committing suicide by jumping into it. The King lamented that such a mass suicide was due to him and he also made a fire-pit and jumped into it.

The heat of the fire-pit woke him from his day-dream and Gādhi found himself in the pond where he had come to bathe. "What! Who am I? What all roles did I take just now?" These puzzling thoughts filled him and he went back to the *āśrama* and started life as usual. One day an old friend of his came to the *āśrama* and after the daily routine they lay down to sleep. During their conversation Gādhi asked his friend why he had become fleshless and so lean. Then his friend narrated a story exactly similar to the experiences which Gādhi had in the country of Kīra. He added that to atone for the sin of his association with the Caṇḍālas he was conducting *Prayāgasnāna* (bath in Prayāga), *Japa* and *Cāndrāyaṇamahāvrata*. All those things he explained, made him lean.

> Gādhi knew that the story of the guest related to him and he was eager to visit the country of Kīra. When he went to Kīra he saw everything there in the same way as in his dream. Then he realised that it was an exhibition by Viṣṇu of the working of Māyā. Gādhi then renounced everything and went into a cave and started doing penance there. After some years Mahāviṣṇu appeared before him and blessed him.[24]

Who *is* in whose dream and who is *not* in whose dream are issues which retain their elusive quality as we pursue a fleece-like luminous cloud of the world as dream floating in the ocean of a dark night, so dark that it is as if darkness were wrapped up in darkness as it were, "darkness which cannot be penetrated by the point of a needle" and all the while within it the dream shines like an inchoate Himālaya, the "frozen sparkling laughter of Śiva!"

---

24. Vettam Mani, *op. cit.*, pp. 495-96. The story is found in the *Yogavāsiṣṭha*, see Swami Venkatesananda, *The Concise Yoga Vāsiṣṭa*, Albany, NY: State University of New York Press, 1984, pp. 202-07. It has also been discussed by Wendy Doniger O'Flaherty, *Dreams Illusion and Other Realities*, Chicago and London: The University of Chicago Press, 1984, Chapter 4.

7

The World as Daydream

ENOUGH said of the world as a dream; what about the world as a daydream? A daydream has a peculiar quality to it unlike a dream; that the subject is aware of dreaming while daydreaming (a quality it shares with a lucid dream as distinguished from ordinary dreams). And here again the subject has the freedom to abandon oneself to the daydream and go where it takes one, or else to mould it according to one's heart's desire. Indeed, in some texts, human bondage to *saṁsāra* is presented in terms of a daydream rather than a dream:

> If in a *day-dream* a man imagines himself taken, harassed and beaten by an enemy he will suffer from the effects until and unless he dismisses the day-dream. Will he continue to be bound by the enemy after the dream is dismissed with the enemy and his body? So it is with the veil of nescience.[1]

There are however some obvious problems in treating the world as daydream, that is, like an idea. Ramaṇa does declare at one point: "The Universe is only an idea."[2] But obviously it is not the kind of idea one may change at will in an instant. For a system of ideas seems to be involved in the case of the universe:

---

1. Swamī Śrī Ramanānanda Saraswathi, tr., *op. cit.*, p. 153.
2. Paul Brunton, *op. cit.*, p. 64.

> A Swamī asked: I feel toothache. Is it only a thought?
>
> M.: Yes.
>
> D.: Why can I not think that there is no toothache and thus cure myself?
>
> M.: When engrossed in other thoughts one does not feel the toothache. When one sleeps toothache is not felt.
>
> D.: But toothache remains all the same.
>
> M.: Such is the firm conviction of the reality of the world that it is not easily shaken off. The world does not become for that reason any more real than the individual himself.
>
> D.: Now there is the Sino-Japanese war. If it is only in imagination, can or will Śrī Bhagavān imagine the contrary and put an end to the war?
>
> M.: The Bhagavān or the questioner is as much a thought as the Sino-Japanese war. (Laughter.)[3]

However, in some texts, the suggestion is made that thoughts can change the universe if they are sustained; indeed if sufficiently sustained they can change the world. The account in which a sage's son abducts the sacrificial horse of a king was narrated early in the book. The king's brother, searching of the sacrificial horse, finds himself lost in a universe within "the circuit of a hill two miles and a half." The passage contains a progression of imagery from a daydream to a dream, as if after a point one becomes the victim of one's own imagination — when a daydream turns into a dream or, well, a nightmare! The passage bears repeating:

> One starts imagining something; then contemplates it; and by continuous or repeated association resolves that it is true unless contradicted. In that way, the world appears real in the manner one is used to it. My world that you

---

3. *Talks with Śrī Ramaṇa Maharṣi*, p. 427.

visited furnishes the proof thereof; come now, let us go round the hill and see.

Saying so, the sage's son took the king, and went round the hill and returned to the former spot.

Then he continued: Look, O King! the circuit of the hill is hardly two miles and a half and yet you have seen a universe within it. Is it real or false? Is it a dream or otherwise? What has passed as a day in that land, has counted for twelve thousand years here, which is correct? Think, and tell me. Obviously you cannot distinguish this from a dream and cannot help concluding that the world is nothing but imagination. My world will disappear instantly if I cease contemplating it.

Therefore convince yourself of the dream-like nature of the world and do not indulge in grief at your brother's death.

Just as the dream creations are pictures moving on the mind screens, so also this world including yourself is the obverse of the picture depicted by pure intelligence and it is nothing more than an image in a mirror. See how you will feel after this conviction. Will you be elated by the accession of a dominion or depressed by the death of a relative in your dream?

Realise that the Self is the self-contained mirror projecting and manifesting this world. The Self is pure unblemished consciousness. Be quick! Realise it quickly and gain transcendental happiness![4]

Yet this need not always be the case. A universe can be projected consciously in a planned and sustained way and precipitated into reality. This is how the sage's son explains the failure of Mahāsena to create anything by his will, in contrast to Brahmā's success in the same venture.

---

4. *Ibid.*, pp. 100-01.

The will conceives either effectively or ineffectively according as it is uniform or broken up by indecision.

Do you not know this world to be the result of Brahmā's desire? This looks real and permanent because the original desire is so powerful.

One should forget the old associations in order to make one's new conception effective and this endures only so long as it is not obstructed by the antecedent one and thus destroyed. It is effective only when forceful; in that way even great things may be achieved.

Your conceptions do not materialise for the aforesaid reason. Therefore you must practise focussing of thought if you desire your own creations to endure.

I shall tell you now about the difference in time and space. You are not proficient in the affairs of the world, and therefore you are mystified. I shall now make it clear how these differences appear. . . . Instances like these are innumerable. Their explanation is as follows:

Sight is of the eye and cannot be without it. A jaundiced eye sees everything yellow and myopia produces the double image of a single object.

Abnormal visions are thus the direct result of abnormal eyes. The Karandakas, in an Eastern island, are said to see everything red; so also the inhabitants of Ramaṇaka isle see everything upside down. One hears many more strange stories of the kind, all of which are based on abnormalities of vision. They can all be remedied by proper treatment. The same applies to other senses including the mind. The relation between space and objects and between time and events is according to your estimate of them; there is no intrinsic relationship between them.[5]

This blurring of lines between daydreaming and dreaming

5. *Ibid.*, p. 103.

has its counterpart in modern dream research in the distinction between NREM or non-rapid-eye-movement sleep and REM or rapid-eye-movement sleep. It is acknowledged now that constant mental activity characterises "night life"[6] or what might be otherwise called "a night of constant dreaming"[7] but it is not always clear to people how to distinguish thinking from dreaming in this process. According to one suggestion, only *REM* periods involve dreaming:

> NREM sleep, by contrast, is sometimes referred to as "orthodox" sleep. While awakenings from it do not normally result in vivid, detailed dream reports, the mind is far from blank at these times. NREM dream reports tend to be shorter, less visual, and less vivid than those reported from REM periods, and subjects often feel themselves to have been thinking rather than dreaming. For this reason, many investigators refer to mental content reported from NREM periods as "thinking" to distinguish it from the real "dreams" of the REM period. However, this is a moot point, and there are those who argue that any mental activity reported on waking from sleep merits the label "dreaming."[8]
>
> However, on the other hand the researcher Goodenough also found that many subjects, notably those who rarely recalled dreams spontaneously at home, seemed to mislabel their dream experiences. One sleeper, aroused during an unmistakable REM period, reported that he had been "asleep and thinking," while others were not sure whether they had been "asleep and dreaming" or "awake and thinking." The difficulty of distinguishing between "dreaming" and "thinking" was a real one for many subjects. One man said he felt he was riding down an avenue and was conscious of

6. Ann Faraday, *Dream Power,* New York: Berkeley Books, 1980, p. 28.
7. *Ibid.*
8. *Ibid.*, pp. 24-25.

> the houses and buildings passing by. He stated, "I may have thought that or dreamed it." Another subject, with a similar difficulty, concluded he must have been dreaming, not thinking, as the events of the "dream" were unreal and inconsistent with the facts of everyday life.[9]

As a matter of fact, an interesting convergence between modern dream research and the Advaitic use of it as a metaphor is provided by the degree of "engrossment" involved in the process of dreaming. Ramaṇa remarks, for instance,

> . . . the dream as a dream does not permit you to doubt its reality. It is the same in the waking state, for you are unable to doubt the reality of the world which you see while you are awake. How can the mind which has itself created the world accept it as unreal? That is the significance of the comparison made between the world of the waking state and the dream-world. *Both are creations of the mind and, so long as the mind is engrossed in either, it finds itself unable to deny their reality* . . .[10]

Ann Faraday also remarks that the "high waking threshold of REM sleep . . . indicates that, in one way at least, it is a state of deep sleep. It has been suggested *that the sleeper is so engrossed in his dreams in* REM sleep that only a very strong stimulus reaches him."[11] If the intention of the Advaitic metaphor of the world as dream is what Ramaṇa states it to be, then, from the standpoint of Advaita, only REM dreams may properly be so called. This leads us into the realm of modern dream research.

---

9. *Ibid.*, p. 38.
10. David Godman, ed., *op. cit.*, p. 189, emphasis added. This passage has also been cited earlier.
11. Ann Faraday, *op. cit.*, p. 24, emphasis added.

8

The World as Dream
Implications of Modern Dream Research

MODERN researches in dream add to the intrigue of the metaphor of the "world as a dream." It enables one to combine, though some might say mix, metaphors — such as that of a dream and a play. Thus in what is called the D-state, which "many researchers go even further in calling. . . the third state of existence; a state in many ways as different from the ordinary sleep (the S-state) as it is from waking,"[1] the rapid eye movements or REM's "were binocularly synchronous, that is, both eyes moved in the same direction as if the sleeper were watching a play."[2] Indeed:

> One of the researchers likened the sleeper, as he is about to enter a REM period, to a spectator at the theatre. Before the curtain rises, he shuffles and fidgets in his seat. As the curtain goes up, he becomes still and attentive. The play begins and he follows the action with his eyes: he becomes excited as the plot unfolds, his breathing speeds up, and his heart thumps. As long as the play continues, he is wholly immersed in it, unmoving and unspeaking (sleep-walking and talking normally take place in Stage 2 sleep). When the curtain falls, he moves and stretches, and his former bodily composure is regained. To the early investigators, the

1. *Ibid.*
2. *Ibid.*, p. 22.

> analogy seemed almost too good to be true: the sleeper could indeed be watching a play during his periods of REM sleep, but a play of his own making in which he himself was the director, producer, stage manager, principal actor, and audience all at the same time. He must, it seemed obvious, be dreaming.[3]

This picture, of course, corresponds closely, if not exactly, to the Advaitic view of the world as dream. The description of this state by Calvin Hall approximate the Advaitic view that we live in a dream-world very closely. According to him:

> A dream is a succession of images, predominantly visual in quality, which are experienced during sleep. A dream commonly has one or more scenes, several characters in addition to the dreamer, and a sequence of actions and interactions usually involving the dreamer. It resembles a motion picture or dramatic production in which the dreamer is both a participant and an observer. Although a dream is a hallucination, since the events of a dream do not actually take place, the dreamer experiences it as though he were seeing something real.[4]
>
> Similarly, two conclusions which Hall drew about dreams seem to be on all fours with the Advaitic view of "the world as dream":

1. The dream is a creation of the dreamer's own mind and tells him how he sees himself, others, the world, his impulses, and so on. It should never be read as a guide to objective reality — that it does not give us the truth about things, but merely a picture of how they appear to us.

---

3. *Ibid.*, p. 23.
4. Quoted, *Ibid.*, pp. 36-37.

2. The dreamer is responsible for everything that appears in his dream. If he dreams something, however terrible or stupid, he must first have thought of it.[5]

There are some elements of this in Jung when he suggests that one should "see the dream elements and characters as aspects of the dreamer's own personality rather than as memories of objective events"[6] but this lacks the forthrightness of Hall's position. For instance, a subject dreamt walking happily with a girl until a crack opened in the earth, which first swallowed her and then him. His girl friend had just informed him that she was pregnant, a pregnancy he wanted terminated. Now:

> if we accept Hall's dictum that the dreamer is the sole author of his dream and is responsible for all that happens in it, then obviously the subject wanted to destroy the girl for not "going along with him" over the abortion, for he caused her to fall down the precipice. Probably as a self-punishment for such a wish, he then brought about his own demise in the dream.[7]

If this point of the sole authorship of one's dream is transferred to the Advaitic view of the world as dream, it shows the doctrine of *karma* in a totally new light. The doctrine, in its standard version, emphasizes individual responsibility to the hilt. All that happens to us we do to us. This point of the doctrine is easily understood if we are the sole author of our dreams. Consider, for instance, the following passage of the *Adhyātma-Rāmāyaṇa* in the light of this view:

---

5. *Ibid.*, pp. 132-33.
6. *Ibid.*, p. 112.
7. *Ibid.*, pp. 137-38.

The Karma

None can ever be the cause of fortune or misfortune of another. The karma which we have ourselves accumulated in the past, that alone is the cause of fortune and misfortune. To attribute one's fortune and misfortune to another is an error, as it is a vain pride to think: "It is I who am the author of this," for all beings are bound by the chain of their karma. If man fancies to himself that some beings are his friends, others his enemies or are indifferent to him, it is according to the karma that he has worked out himself. It is necessary, therefore, that man should bear with one mind his fortune and misfortune, which are only fruits of his own actions. He should say unto himself: "I desire neither to obtain enjoyments nor to be deprived of them; whether I acquire them or not, it is just the same"; and thus he should not be a slave. In whatever situation, whatever time, and for whatever reasons, man accomplishes an action, good or bad, he must submit to its consequences accordingly.

It is therefore in vain he rejoices or is aggrieved of a happy or an unhappy event, because the decrees of Destiny are inevitable even for demons and gods. Man can never escape pleasure or pain, because his body, which is a product of his good or bad actions, is by nature transient. After pleasure pain, after pain pleasure: creatures cannot escape these two, as they cannot the succession of day and night. They are intimately associated as water and mud. It is, therefore, that Sages knowing that all is but illusion, remain steadfast and neither are aggrieved nor joyous for events unhappy or happy.[8]

Upon reading this passage one might wonder why, if we create our own dreams, do we include unpleasant experiences

---

8. Louis Renou, ed., *Hinduism,* New York: George Braziller, 1962, p. 197.

in them. It is here that Jung's concept of the shadow archetype[9] may be of some help. For if, as Jung believed, wholeness could not be attained by "escaping from the shadow (which is impossible) but by integrating this rejected part of the personality" into our life-style, then one can see not only why all our dreams will not be dreams of elysium but, if our existence now itself is a dream, how it might alternate between living in heaven, hell and this earth. The Advaitic idea that we may all be dreaming the same dream also seems relevant in the context of archetypes.

The Gestalt approach to dreams helps come to grip with another aspect of the Advaitic view of "the world as dream." One of the issues raised in the context of the Advaitic analysis of the triple stream of existence or *avasthātraya* is the following. If we equate, or even compare, the waking state to the dream state, how do we account for the relative consistency of the waking state from day to day compared to the dream state, which lacks such consistency. The issue is a standard one in Advaitic text. In the following passage a philosophical answer is also incorporated:

> Do you contend that the waking state is not so because there is continuity in it after you wake up? Is there no continuity in your dreams from day to day?
>
> If you say that it is not evident, tell me whether the continuity in the wakeful world is not broken up every moment of your life.
>
> Do you suggest that the hills, the seas and the earth itself are really permanent phenomena, in spite of the fact that their appearance is constantly changing? Is not the dream-

9. Jolande Jacobi, *Complex Archetype Symbol in the Psychology of C.G. Jung*, Princeton: Princeton University Press, 1959, p. 114, etc.

> world also similarly continuous with its earth, mountains, rivers, friends and relatives?
>
> Do you still doubt its abiding nature? Then extend the same reasoning to the nature of the wakeful world and know it to be equally evanescent.
>
> The ever-changing objects like the body, trees, rivers, and islands are easily found to be transitory. Even mountains are not immutable, for their contours change owing to the erosion of waterfalls and mountain torrents; thunder; lightning and storms; and so on. You will observe similar changes in the seas and on earth.
>
> Therefore I tell you that you should investigate the matter closely.[10]

The answer, though useful, is not entirely satisfactory. It answers the question by generalizing the issue — it does not address its specificity. Ramaṇa also sometimes takes resource to such a procedure. But if we explain normal life on "the world as dream" metaphor as a *recurring* dream, then Ann Faraday's assessment of the Gestalt approach becomes fascinating in this context. She writes: "It has been my experience that the totally subjective Gestalt approach, taking all dream elements as aspects of the dreamer's personality, is particularly valuable with recurring dreams, since they are likely to *reflect long-standing conflicts* triggered off from time to time by some relevant external situation."[11] Inasmuch as our lives are made of ongoing conflicts, the fact of the recurring nature of the daily world even on the "world as dream" view becomes more plausible. There are points where Ann Faraday

---

10. Swami Sri Ramanananda Saraswathi, tr., *op. cit.*, pp. 98-99. This passage has been cited earlier.
11. Ann Faraday, *op. cit.*, p. 145.

insists on the link between the dream and the dreamer, as when she says: "that the dream is the property of the dreamer, a unique production arising out of his own vast network of memories and associations, and, in the end of the day, is meaningful in whatever way he himself finds most useful."[12] Or when she insists on every dreamer's right to insist on the reality of his own dream experience, she sounds very Advaitin, although writing out of modern psychological research on dreams.

The fact that life is experienced as fragmentary is a well-known fact. In fact it has given rise to the waggish remark: "Just when you think you've got the big picture, someone changes the channel"! Curiously enough, the view of "the world as dream" may help explain this randomness about life, without implying the lack of interconnectedness of any kind whatsoever. Thus:

> whenever we see an object, witness an event, or think a thought a whole train of ideas is set in motion which do not seem to be connected in any logical fashion. For example, when I look at a tree and am reminded of the lilac tree in the garden of my childhood home, my mind may jump to a school friend called Lila Carlton, to memories of holidays together in Yorkshire, to the first sexual experiments, and so on. All this can go on without my conscious knowledge and may appear later in a dream as *a strange cluster of apparently unrelated events*.[13]

This can give a new sense to the expression that life does not make sense. Consider the fact that when "external stimulation is withdrawn during sleep and waking logic disappears, . . .

---

12. *Ibid.*, p. 291.

13. *Ibid.*, p. 88, emphasis added.

trains of association may appear openly in a dream" — or on the view of "the world as dream" even in our normal daily life. The line, to be sure, has to be drawn somewhere in pursuing this line of reasoning but one is not sure where. Consider the following dream sequence:

> As I was drifting off to sleep, he wrote, "I saw those coloured balls of this afternoon's film rolling toward me. This led me to think of chocolate rolls and of woman's role in society. It was, of course, to roll her hips and I immediately found H. standing before me in the dream rolling her hips in a very seductive manner. This led me straight into a sex dream about her."[14]

Should we not consider the possibility that this could as well have transpired in "real" life considering the strange ways people get turned on in real life? In this approach one could perhaps define Karma as "how the thoughts of a person are tied together"![15] And if we accept the possibility of the world and our life in it being a dream or as a dream, the Talmudic pronouncement: "A dream is its own interpretation"[16] — takes on new meaning.

One must also here consider the phenomenon of being awakened *by* a dream. If the Advaitic world-view — the view of "the world as a dream" is accepted as also its Advaitic corollary, that one should wake up from this dream, the question arises: how is this brought about? One Advaitic answer among others has been that the dream itself can wake one up — as often happens in a nightmare. This could be one reason why suffering is not taken that seriously in Advaita —

---

14. *Ibid.*, p. 90.
15. *Ibid.*, p. 133.
16. *Ibid.*, p. 117.

not because the sufferer does not at least ostensibly suffer — but that intense suffering has the property of catapulting one out of the world of suffering itself, just as a nightmare removes the very suffering it is inflicting when its horror wakes one up.

This experience of being awakened *from* the dream *by* the dream itself is mentioned even by Freud:

> It not infrequently happens to me, as well as to other analysts and to patients under treatment, that, having been woken up, as one might say, by a dream, I immediately afterwards, and in full possession of my intellectual powers, set about interpreting it. In such cases, I have often refused to rest till I have arrived at a complete understanding of the dream: yet it has sometimes been my experience that after finally waking up in the morning, I have entirely forgotten both my interpretive activity and the content of the dream, though knowing that I have had a dream and interpreted it. It happens far more often that the dream draws the findings of my interpretive activity back with it into oblivion than that my intellectual activity succeeds in preserving the dream in my memory.[17]

The nightmare is only a dramatic example of what might appear less dramatically, even spontaneously and this would provide an interesting parallel to cases of spontaneous Realization in Advaita — as in the case of Ramaṇa.

If Freud could forget his dream, is it possible that instead of remembering their past lives the Advaitin sages *forget* them? For curiously, in contrast with Buddhism, there is little talk of recalling past lives among Advaitin elites. Freud, in upholding the view of the "psychoanalyst independent of the dreamer

---

17. Quoted in Ann Faraday, *Ibid.*, p. 57.

who could overcome the dreamer's psychological resistance to seeing the truth"[18] also conjures up the figure of the Guru in Advaita who cuts through the Gordian knots of his disciples with the sword of knowledge with, however, this major difference that this entire process itself is regarded as ultimately illusory in Advaita,[19] and the disciple and Master are not just equal but non-dual.

The analysis of dream in modern psychology and physiology thus enriches the world as dream metaphor considerably — and at times expectedly; but by the same token it also demonstrates its limitation. For instance, the conceptualization of world as a dream is ultimately directed towards establishing its unreality; and that too, an unreality of a particular kind, its *objective* unreality. The whole irony of the following statement of the *Tripurā-Rahasya* is based on this fact: "Just as a dreamer is foolishly alarmed at his *own* dreams. . . ."[20] And this in turn only a reflection of a more fundamental metaphysical statement about the "unknowability . . . of a knower outside of consciousness."[21]

In modern dream research, however, the link with objective reality, although it may become tenuous, is never snapped. Ann Faraday would therefore maintain that "while dreams are concerned with what the dreamer thinks and feels about various people and events, they can sometimes be found on examination to reveal some objective truth which either the dreamer or the person he dreams about have been trying to

---

18. *Ibid.*, p. 97.
19. William Cenkner, *A Tradition of Teachers: Śaṅkara and the Jagadgurus Today*, Delhi: Motilal Banarsidass, 1983, p. 57.
20. Swami Sri Ramananda Saraswathi, tr., *op. cit.*, p. 97.
21. *Ibid.*, p. 115.

avoid in waking life."[22] In fact, while discussing Hall's approach to dreams, this is one way in which Ann Faraday distinguishes her own position from his, and she reverts to the same point later on in the book. Thus, by way of contradistinction from Hall's *interpretive* approach she states: "I prefer to tackle a dream in the first instance as a picture of some objective event which has escaped the dreamer's notice during waking life. I have found during the course of my work that dreams can sometimes be extremely useful in bringing to our attention facts we have brushed aside during the day either because we do not want to face them or because we were too busy at the time really to notice them."[23] And subsequently she observes that in some cases:

> The dream may provide us with very valuable information about the external world, and it is for this reason that I believe we should examine all dreams for elements of objective reality. These may act as reminders, warnings, of even predictions, and I feel it is as foolish to ignore this possibility as it is to make the opposite mistake of seeing all dream events as accurate revelations of real people or situations.[24]

All this is, of course, unexceptionable if we accept the standard doctrine of the *three* levels of reality — the *pāramārthika*, the *vyāvahārika* and the *prātibhāsika*. But part of the point of developing the concept of "the world as dream", for at least *some* Advaitins, is to reduce this trichotomy in *effect* to a dichotomy. Ramaṇa alludes to this when he remarks: "If Reality be used in the wider sense the world may be said to have the

---

22. Ann Faraday, *op. cit.*, p. 136.
23. *Ibid.*, p. 141.
24. *Ibid.*, p. 160.

everyday life and illusory degrees (*vyāvahārika* and *prātibhāsika satya*). Some, however, deny even the reality of practical life — *vyāvahārika satya* and consider it to be only projection of the mind. According to them it is only *prātibhāsika satya*, i.e., an illusion."[25] Such an Advaitic view of the "world as dream" could never suggest that dreams "often bring to our attention things we have failed to notice in waking life."[26]

The explanation of these limitations of course lies in the simple fact that modern dream analysis is conducted *within* the context of the world, while in Advaita the dream-metaphor is used to illuminate the context of the world *itself*. This becomes clear when we consider Freud's understanding of a dream as wish fulfilment — that "*the motive of a dream was a wish and its content was the fulfilment of a wish*."[27] One should, however, not confuse the word wish here as we use it in "wishful thinking." For if we take the word wish in the wishful sense we are hard put to explain why our dreams are not always happy *or* on the view of the "world as dream," why our lives in this world are not of uninterrupted felicity as we would like them to be. Wishes are psychic acts with consequences — both in Freud and in Advaita. In this context the famous Irma dream, which gave rise to the idea of dream as wish-fulfilment — a point on which Freudian and Advaitin analyses could converge in their own contexts — also illustrates the vast difference which yawns between these two contexts. Freud's account of the Irma dream runs as follows. In 1895:

> He was sitting on the terrace of the Bellevue hotel in Vienna pondering a dream of the previous night in which a

---

25. *Talks with Śrī Ramaṇa Maharṣi*, p. 43.

26. Ann Faraday, *op. cit.*, p. 16.

27. *Ibid.*, p. 69.

> hysterical patient of his, Irma, told him she still had pains and was far from cured. She looked so ill in the dream that Freud became alarmed and thought he must have overlooked some organic sickness. His colleagues in the dream reached the same conclusion and said she was suffering from an infection as a result of an injection administered by Freud's friend Otto with a dirty syringe.
>
> The dream had obviously been sparked off by the fact that on the evening before the dream, Otto had actually visited Freud and told him that he had seen Irma on holiday and that she looked better but not well. Freud thought he detected a note of reproach in Otto's voice and carried over his anxieties into sleep.[28]

Now Freud remarks:

> The dream fulfilled certain wishes which were started in me by the events of the previous evening. . . . The conclusion of the dream... was that I was not responsible for the persistence of Irma's pains, but that Otto was. Otto had in fact annoyed me by his remarks about Irma's incomplete cure, and the dream gave me my revenge by throwing back the reproach on him. The dream acquitted me of the responsibility for Irma's condition by showing that it was due to other factors. . . . The dream represented a particular state of affairs as I should have wished it to be.[29]

If, in Freud's statement, the word "evening" is replaced by *past life* then the discussion can be plugged into the Advaitic world-view. It may be recalled that in Advaita daily sleep is compared as daily death (*dainandina maraṇam*)[30] and death is compared to sleep: "Death is intervening sleep between two

---

28. *Ibid.*, p. 68.
29. Quoted, *ibid*.
30. P. Sankaranarayanan, *op. cit.*, p. 35.

successive births while sleep intervenes between two *jāgrat*s [waking states] and both are transient."[31] The important point to recognize in the case of both dreams in ordinary life and dream as a metaphor for ordinary life is that in either case "dreams are not just things that *happen* . . . out of the blue, but fantasies. . . [we ourselves] act out . . . in order to tell [ourselves] something of importance."[32]

Another limitation of the Advaitic metaphor of the world as dream may be identified somewhat curiously. One must here first recognize that according to the Advaitin our daily life offers many glimpses of ultimate reality although full-fledged Samādhi or Realization is experienced by the chosen few. An early text identifies the following:

> instances of that state: when a man remains unaware of "in and out" for a short interval and is not overpowered by the ignorance of sleep; the infinitesimal time when one is beside one-self with joy; when embraced by one's beloved in all purity; when a thing is gained which was intensely longed for but given up in despair; when a lonely traveller moving with the utmost confidence is suddenly confronted with the utmost danger; when one hears of the sudden death of one's only son, who was in the best of health, in the prime of life, and at the apex of his glory. . . . There are also intervals of Samādhi, namely the interim period between the waking, dream and sleep states; at the time of sighting a distant object, the mind holding the body at one end projects itself into space until it holds the objects at the other end, just as a worm prolongs itself at the time of leaving one hold to catch another hold. Carefully watch the state of mind in the interval.[33]

31. Paul Brunton and Munagala Venkataramiah, *op. cit.*, pp. 72, 93.
32. Ann Faraday, *op. cit.*, p. 272.
33. Swami Sri Ramanananda Saraswathi, tr., *op. cit.*, pp. 130-31.

In fact it is claimed that:

> the wakeful sleep is iridescent with fleeting Samādhi and sleep. Men when they are awake can detect fleeting sleep because they are already conversant with its nature. But fleeting Samādhi goes undetected because people are not so conversant with it. O Brāhmaṇa! Fleeting Samādhi is indeed being experienced by all, even in their busy moments; but it passes unnoticed by them, for want of acquaintance with it.[34]

It appears that the kind of alteration in state of consciousness which accompanies any alteration in state of consciousness, and is identified as fleeting Samādhi, may also occur during dreams, if physiological evidence is any guide. Thus research indicates that body movements during sleep "are responsible for breaking an ongoing dream and starting a new one within the same REM period, in much the same way as a sudden disturbance in everyday life brings us out of one reverie, either into another or back to reality."[35]

These observations seem to establish the possibility of fleeting Samādhi during dream, though not recognized as such. However, it is at this point that the metaphor breaks down. Although the waking state is compared to a dream according to the Advaitic metaphor, Realization is not possible in a dream, according to received doctrine, but it is possible in the waking state,[36] which has been compared to the dream in these pages.

The juxtaposition of the Advaitic metaphor of the dream as a way to refer to the world and the results of the experimental research in the modern world produce another

34. *Ibid.*, p. 129.

35. Ann Faraday, *op. cit.*, p. 43.

36. Paul Brunton and Munagala Venkataramiah, *op. cit.*, pp. 130-31.

curious result. This relates to the relative roles of dreaming and waking and the world as dreaming, and Realization as an Awakening from it. At one point in her book, Ann Faraday asks a question and answers it as well, as follows: "Does the nightly dance of day memories and their associations have any psychological value for us if we do not become aware of them through waking? If it does, then perhaps it would be better to let it get on with its work without interruption, just like the goblins in fairy tales who spring-clean the house at night as long as they remain unobserved."[37] Quite obviously a host of researchers from Freud onwards in modern times are of the view that dreams have meaning from the point of view of our waking state,[38] though an opposite point of view has also been voiced.[39] On balance, however, it is clear that at least in our own times dreams are significant not only qua dreams but also as related to the world, but the "dream" experience has no significance for the Awakening in Advaita except in so far as the "dream" experience may have provoked it. Sometimes this is expressed in theistic form, as in the following exchange with Ramaṇa.

> D.: Why does God permit suffering in the world? Should He not with His omnipotence do away with it at one stroke and ordain the universal realization of God?
>
> M.: Suffering is the way for Realization of God.
>
> D.: Should He not ordain differently?
>
> M.: It is the way.[40]

But sometimes it is also spelt out in Advaitic starkness.

---

37. *Ibid.*, p. 129.

38. *Ibid.*, p. 66 ff.

39. *Ibid.*, p. 80.

40. *Ibid.*, pp. 26, 30, 52, 70, 77 ff, 81, 82 ff, 87, 102, 218.

> Q. *Why did the Self manifest as this miserable world?*
>
> A. In order that you might seek it. Your eyes cannot see themselves. Place a mirror before them. Then only they see themselves. Similarly with creation. See yourself first and then see the whole world as the Self.[41]

Self-revelation as the world of dream is for the revelation of the Self. The dream world is what is left behind — not what is carried into the Awakening by contrast with normal living in which dream states may bear messages, like Hermes, for the waking state.

Yet another limitation of the application of modern dream researches to the metaphor of "world as dream" would arise if we were to argue that dream experiences may have meaningfulness in their own right — apart from their connection to the state of waking. It is easy to see why this would be valid if we viewed empirical existence as consisting of three distinct states of consciousness — waking, dreaming and deep sleep. But if the *entire* range of empirical existence is equated with dreaming, as is the case with the metaphor of the world as dream — then the true significance of dream only lies in the context of waking from it and the following remarks about certain dreams do not apply here:

> certain dreams should not necessarily be valued only in terms of any psychological insight or creative inspiration we might bring back from them to waking life, but also as experiences in their own right. For why should not our dream life, like our waking life, contain experiences that are ends in themselves — like looking at beautiful landscapes or pictures, listening to music, talking to people, and making love — rather than merely means to something else? After

41. *Ibid.*, p. 163.

> all, nature has been generous with our dream time, and we can surely — in spite of our Protestant ethic — allow ourselves a little of that time for pure, unadulterated aesthetic pleasure.[42]

The simultaneous investigation of the Advaitic view of the world as dream, and modern researches in the phenomenon of dream, produce surprising and occasionally even exciting results. For instance, one finds oneself teased by the possibility of at least four conceptual bridges which could be possibly thrown over the waters which separate them: two of these from the Advaitic shore and two from the other.

One of the interesting concepts in Advaita is that of Karma, especially of Karma being without a beginning (*anādi*). The more complex understanding of Karma made possible by modern dream research was identified in the preceding sections, when it was hinted how Karma could possibly and profitably be understood as "how the thoughts of a person are tied together."[43] But the concept of Karma as *anādi* somehow seems more elusive. Modern psychological developments nevertheless seem to place it more within one's grasp. Ann Faraday analyzes one of her dreams in which her mother does not come out in a good light. But she hastens to add: "I am not blaming my mother for my problems: the blaming game leads nowhere except away from the problem, for she could in turn blame her own mother and so on ad infinitum."[44] Could not the idea of considering Karma as *anādi* reflect a similar realization? One could blame one's condition on past Karma, and that Karma on even more remote Karma till the chain of "causation" disappeared in the mists of ever-receding lives!

---

42. Ann Faraday, *op. cit.*, p. 303.

43. *Ibid.*, p. 133.

44. *Ibid.*, p. 257.

This sandwich may have more meat in it than is apparent at first sight, for in the Ṛgvedic period Karma was indeed seen as passing from generation to generation — a concept of whose existence we are still reminded by the Hindu memorial rite of *śrāddha*, despite attempts to integrate it which a later view in which Karma was passed on not so much from generation to generation as from one birth to another. In fact one might ask why the *dual* operation is not explicitly recognized in Hindu thought, as they need not necessarily be mutually exclusive. In any case, the point here is that whether one blames one's parents, or one's Karma, the ball will never stop rolling back. The thing to do is to pick it up and start playing the game.

The other Advaitic idea which seems to possess a bridge-building possibility is the distinction drawn within Advaita between the Self and the not-Self. Great emphasis is laid on distinguishing the Self from the not-Self (*ātmānātmaviveka*) in Advaita. The following verses of *Vivekacūḍāmaṇi* may be cited on this point. In the first verse cited (no. 122) the not-Self is described; in the next the Self (no. 125) and then the consequence of misidentifying the two, in the third verse (no. 137).

Verse 122

> The body, organs, *prāṇas*, *manas*, egoism, etc. all modifications, the sense-objects, pleasure, and the rest, the gross elements such as the ether, in fact, the whole universe, up to the Undifferentiated — all this is the non-Self.
>
> [This and the next Śloka set forth what we are to avoid identifying ourselves with. We are the Pure Self, eternally free from all duality.][45]

---

45. Swami Madhavananda, *op. cit.*, p. 46.

Verse 125

> There is some Absolute Entity, the *eternal substratum of the consciousness of egoism*, the witness of the three states, and distinct from the five sheaths* or coverings:
>
> [*Five sheaths, etc. — Consisting respectively of Anna (matter), *Praṇā* (force), *Mana*s (mind), *Vijñāna* (knowledge) and *Ānanda* (Bliss). The first comprises this body of ours, the next three make up the subtle body (Sūkṣma Śarīra), and the last the causal body (Kārana Śarīra). *The Ātman referred to in this Śloka is beyond them all.* These *Kośa*s (sheaths) will be dealt with later on.][46]

Verse 137

> Identifying the Self with this non-Self — this is the bondage of man, which is due to his ignorance, and brings in its train the miseries of birth and death. It is through this that one considers this evanescent body as real, and identifying oneself with it, nourishes, bathes, and preserves it by means of (agreeable) sense-objects, by which he becomes bound as the caterpillar by the threads of its cocoon.[47]

A more modern translation of these verses runs as follows:

> The body, the sense organs, the breath, the mind, the sense of "I," all modifications, the sense objects, pleasures, gross elements such as the sky, the entire universe up to the unmanifested, all this is the not-self.
>
> There is something which always exists by itself as the substratum of one's "I"-awareness. It is the witness of the three states and is distinct from the five sheaths.

---

46. *Ibid.*, p. 47, emphasis added.
47. *Ibid.*, p. 52. The modern translation which follows is from John Grimes, *The Vivekacūḍāmaṇi of Śaṅkarācārya Bhagavatpāda*, Hants, England: Ashgate Publishing Company, 2004, pp. 117, 118, 124.

> Solely believing that the not-self is the self is the cause of the individual's bondage. This belief arises from ignorance. It is the cause of being completely engulfed by birth, death, the afflictions and so on. It is because of this that one thinks the unreal body is real and, identifying with it, one nourishes, bathes, and protects it by sense objects, thereby becoming bound like the silkworm in its own woven cocoon.

This misidentification of the Self with the not-Self is thus said to be the metaphysical root of our existential suffering which envelopes life, and the realization of the distinction is crucial to the resolution of the situation.

An equally interesting point about the situation, however, is that in reality the *Self includes* the not-Self. It is the confusion between the two — the lack of differentiation which is the root of the problem. Thus after Realization the not-Self does not disappear — only the true relationship between the Self and the not-Self is recognized. Ramaṇa when explicitly asked: "*Viveka* is said to be discrimination between the Self and the non-Self. What is the non-Self?,"[48] replies:

> M.: There is no non-self, in fact. The non-self also exists in the Self. It is the Self which speaks of the non-self because it has forgotten itself. Having lost hold of itself, it conceives something as non-self, which is after all nothing but itself.[49]

This is rendered somewhat clearer when Ramaṇa explains Śaṅkara's position. It should be borne in mind in reading the passage that *anātman*, or not-Self, belongs to *Māyā* (*Vivekacūḍāmaṇi*, verse 123):

> Śaṅkara also said that this world is Brahman or the Self. What he objected to is one's imagining that the Self is limited

48. *Talks with Śrī Ramaṇa Maharṣi*, p. 269.
49. *Ibid.*, p. 270.

> by the names and forms that constitute the world. He only said that the world has no reality apart from Brahman. Brahman or the Self is like a cinema screen and the world like the pictures on it. You can see the picture only so long as there is a screen. But when the observer himself becomes the screen only the Self remains.
>
> Śaṅkara has been criticized for his philosophy of *Māyā* (illusion) without understanding his meaning. He made three statements; the Brahman is real, that the universe is unreal, and that Brahman is the Universe. He did not stop with the second. The third statement explains the first two; it signifies that when the Universe is perceived apart from Brahman, that perception is false and illusory. What it amounts to is that phenomena are real when experienced as the Self, and illusory when seen apart from the Self.
>
> The Self alone exists and is real. The world, the individual and God are, like the illusory appearance of silver in the mother-of-pearl, imaginary creations in the Self. They appear and disappear simultaneously. Actually, the Self alone is the world, the "I" and God. All that exists is only a manifestation of the Supreme.[50]

When one turns to some aspects of dream research, armed with double insight (1) that the differentiation between not-Self and Self is vital for Realization and (2) this Realization includes recognition of their non-difference, then some striking structural parallels between Advaita and some aspects of modern research begin to emerge, as when Ann Faraday writes:

> In fact, whenever dream characters or themes recur, they reflect deeper problems underlying those which concern specific external events or situations. In these more special dreams, the probability is that all the dream images are parts

50. Arthur Osborne, ed., *op. cit.*, pp. 11-12.

> of ourselves, and it is always interesting to discover with which aspects we identify and which aspects we project onto the other dream characters as the "not-I." The meaning of these dreams becomes fully clear only when we allow the characters to encounter the "I" in open dialogue and to "speak for themselves," as recommended by Jung and worked out in more detail by Perls. As I hope to show, the experience of doing so sometimes brings such a flood of new meaning that I am reminded of St. Paul's famous words: "For now we see through a glass, darkly, but then face to face: now I know in part; but then shall I know even as also I am known."[51]

One may now use ideas developed in modern dream studies as the vantage point for developing fresh perspectives on the metaphor of the world as dream. One such idea which seems extremely promising is the concept of the lucid dream. This phenomenon has received increasing attention over the last few decades,[52] especially in researches on dream being carried out at Oxford. But, what, one might begin by asking, is a lucid dream?

> The "lucid" dream is so called not because it is unusually vivid but because the dreamer is aware at the time of dreaming that he is dreaming, and feels himself to be in full possession of what we call normal waking consciousness while knowing himself quite certainly to be asleep in bed. This kind of dream is sometimes called a "dream of knowledge," which, in my view, is a more suitable dramatic title for what is undoubtedly a most dramatic phenomenon.[53]

---

51. Ann Faraday, *op. cit.*, p. 223.
52. See Celia Green, *Lucid Dreams*, Oxford: Institute of Psychophysical Research, 1968.
53. Ann Faraday, *op. cit.*, p. 298.

Once one is aware in a dream that one is dreaming, one's behaviour in the dream can be radically affected by this realization. Here is an account as to how this might conceivably happen. Ann Faraday considers one of these lucid dreams so remarkable that it deserves to be cited in toto:

> It was sparked off by a conversation with a woman anthropologist friend the previous evening, who had heard one of my broadcasts and said she envied my ability to put over my ideas simply to the lay public; she said she could never bring herself to dilute her own ideas sufficiently to do this. At the time, *I detected the implication that my efforts at popularization were not really academically respectable,* but my conscious mind brushed this aside as sour grapes on her part. My unconscious mind, however, was evidently not so happy about it, since that night my dreaming mind confronted me with my own formidable academic topdog, (Professor Macbeth?).
>
> I dreamed I was having dinner with a rather uptight group of psychologists when a woman across the table suddenly started recriminating with me for leaving the world of the academic elite and lowering my standards to those of the Sunday newspapers. I protested that this was an exaggeration, and that I believed the layman was entitled to at least some of our ideas, especially as he was paying for our research. At this, she literally spat across the table that I was bringing the whole profession into disrepute, that we must retain some vestige of authority, and so on. My fury rose to such a pitch that I had an irresistible desire to beat her up, and *no sooner had I become aware of this desire than I realised with the utmost clarity that I was dreaming and could do exactly what I wanted because dream bodies cannot get hurt.*
>
> So, leaning across the table, I grabbed her by the hair, punched her face, and knocked her front teeth out. This inspired me to further violence and with an exhilaration I

> have never previously experienced, I dragged her onto the floor and began to beat up her body in the same way. Of course, she fought back, and I can still feel the slashing of her fingernails across my cheek and the kicks of what felt like hobnailed boots on my back. At last I detected the waning of her strength, and the fight was over. Then the scene changed, and I found myself in another room walking toward this woman, who was now transformed and wearing a nurse's uniform. As we approached each other, I reminded myself that I must not magically change the events of my lucid dream but allow them to happen spontaneously and observe the outcome. I noted that she was smiling now and that her front teeth were back in place. She then put out her arms to me in a friendly gesture, and we hugged each other.[54]

The rest of the account runs as follows:

> I woke up with a great sense of well-being, as if my humanistic underdog had really made its protest against my academic topdog and brought about a Perlsian release of energy through new integration — and I felt it not just in my mind but throughout my whole body in a way that rarely happens in waking Perlsian dialogue, which is mainly a verbal procedure. This discovery of a "dream body" through which physical tension can be released without causing harm to anyone seems to be closely related to the ideas of the Senoi, and also echoes the ancient esoteric notion that lucid dreaming can provide a way into a "fourth state of existence" beyond sleep, in which the individual can build up a "psychic body" capable of transcending ordinary life. Here is a most exciting prospect for further exploration, and the first essential step in this particular area must be to see how far we can train ourselves in the capacity for lucid dreaming. This is something we have begun to study in our

---

54. *Ibid.*, pp. 300-01, emphasis added.

dream groups concurrently with our more down-to-earth concern with dreams as a means of clearing away life's blocks.[55]

The case of lucid dreaming bears direct relevance to Advaitic thought, especially as mediated throughout the metaphor of the world as a dream. This can be established in at least two ways. Firstly, one could maintain that if one *realised* that the dream is just a dream, this would itself represent some kind, or even degree of Realization. It is often said that there are no degrees in Realization — this is true, but from the standpoint of Realization. From the standpoint of the empirical world, someone who realises that the world is a dream is in some sense closer to Reality. Here one must distinguish between *recognising* the world as a dream, and *realising* the world as dream. For instance, the reader of this book may be prepared to accept the plausibility of the view that the world is a dream — that is to say, prepared to recognise it as a dream. But this is quite different from experientially realising it to be so and not be affected by the vicissitudes of life. These two conditions are again different from a third — namely, waking up from the dream, which is Realization. There is a lot of difference between waking up *in* a dream and waking up *from* a dream.

The phenomenon of lucid dream may help us understand some comments made about the life of the Realized one in his post-liberation phase. The Realized one, knowing the world to be a dream in a first-hand sort of way, possesses a freedom in dealing which ordinary mortals don't and which they can only envy. It is helpful to recall here Ann Faraday realizing during her lucid dream *"with the utmost clarity that I was dreaming and could do exactly what I wanted because dream bodies cannot get hurt"* before she went on a physical rampage against her

55. *Ibid.*, pp. 301-02.

colleague. This might help explain the attitude of the Realized one to killing, which must otherwise seem shockingly callous. Ramaṇa remarks for instance:

> For a realised man, the one who remains ever in the Self, the loss of one or several or all lives either in this world or in all the three worlds makes no difference. Even if he happens to destroy them all, no sin can touch such a pure soul. Maharṣi quoted the *Gītā*, Chapter 18, Verse 17 — "He who is free from the notion of ego, whose intellect is unattached, though he annihilates all the worlds, he slayeth not, nor is he bound by the results of his actions."[56]

It is clear that even if we slay vast multitudes *in a dream* we do not incur any guilt. There are no war crimes in dreams. Thus on the world as dream idea — what is involved is the destruction of mere dream bodies and no killing is involved from a metaphysical point of view; and morally no killing is involved because the moral outlook of the Realised one is so different from our own. The problem of killing arises from the point of view of the unrealized:

> An unrealized man sees one who Realized and identifies him with the body. Because he does not know the Self and mistakes the body for the Self, he extends the same mistake to the body of the Realized Man. The latter is therefore considered to be the physical form. Again, the unrealized man, though in fact not the originator of his actions, imagines himself to be so, and considers the actions of the body as his own and therefore thinks the Realized Man to be so acting when the body is active. But the latter knows the truth and is not deceived. His state cannot be understood by the unrealized and therefore the question of his actions troubles the latter although it does not arise for himself.

---

56. *Talks with Śrī Ramaṇa Maharṣi*, pp. 12-13.

> All good or divine qualities are included in *Jñāna* (spiritual Enlightenment) and all bad or Satanic qualities in *ajñāna* (spiritual darkness). When *jñāna* comes all *ajñāna* goes, so that all divine qualities come automatically. If a man is a *Jñānī* he cannot utter lies or commit any sin.[57]

The force of the last line of the quotation cited above must be fully felt: it is not that the Realized one does not just commit sin, such a one *cannot* commit sin because egoism is lost.[58] This naturally raises the following question, to which the answer is also provided.

> Q: Śaṅkara says we are all free, not bound, and that we shall all go back to God from whom we have come as sparks from a fire. Then why should we not commit all sorts of sins?
>
> A: It is true we are not bound and that the real Self has no bondage. It is true that you will eventually go back to your source. But meanwhile, if you commit sins, as you call them, you will have to face the consequences of such sins. You cannot escape them. If a man beats you, then, can you say, "I am free, I am not bound by these beatings and I don't feel any pain. Let him beat on?" If you can feel like that, you can go on doing what you like. What is the use of merely saying with your lips "I am free?"[59]

In other words, there is no point in *pretending* that one realizes the world is a dream, unless one has achieved Realization.

The issue of the impeccability of the Realized is a standard one in Advaita and several attempts have been made to provide a satisfactory answer. Eliot Deutsch remarks:

---

57. Arthur Osborne, *op. cit.*, pp. 244-45.
58. *Ibid.*, p. 243.
59. David Godman, ed., *op. cit.*, pp. 215-16.

> But what about the man who has realized the highest value, who has gone beyond good and evil? Is he justified in committing any kind of act whatsoever? *The logical answer to this is yes; but the psychological answer is no.* According to Advaita, nothing that the realized person, the *jīvanmukta*, does is subject to moral judgment: he is no longer a judge himself, and he cannot be judged by a phenomenal scale of values. Psychologically, however, this does not mean that he could in fact perform certain actions that, from the lower standpoint, would be judged immoral (e.g., murder) because the performance of these actions presupposes egoism, a desire for self-enhancement and the like, on the part of the actor — an egoism that results from a false identification of the self with the body, senses, mind and so forth. And if such egoism or ignorance were present, then the actor could not in fact be the realized sage.[60]

William Indich points out that *mokṣa* transcends *dharma* no doubt, but one has to "bring one's desires in harmony with the universal moral order in preparation for the transcendence of both desire and moral order."[61] But whatever the moral or logical answer, the metaphysical question from the metaphor of the world as dream is clear — is killing dream bodies killing? And the question contains the answer.

Another point established by modern dream research may now be taken into account — that dreaming is a state of consciousness independent of sleeping and waking, a "third state of existence," a formulation consistent with both ancient and standard Hindu thought[62] but relatively new in the West.

---

60. Eliot Deutsch, *op. cit.*, p. 102, emphasis added.
61. William Indich, *op. cit.*, p. 91.
62. Heinrich Zimmer, *Philosophies of India*, New York: Pantheon Books, 1951: edited by Joseph Campbell, p. 374, etc.

The main point is that "our conscious minds are needed if we are to make the most of our dreams; by bringing them into waking consciousness and learning to understand them we may be led to a reappraisal of our whole mode of living."[63] However, we saw earlier the consequences of becoming conscious of dreaming *while* dreaming, as compared with the more ordinary situation of recalling dreams in waking state. Now if we can *achieve* lucid dreams, could one not attain something like *lucid sleep*, by moving waking state consciousness into deep sleep? This is precisely the suggestion made by Ramaṇa at several places, strange and far-fetched as it may sound:

> In the deep sleep state we lay down our ego (Ahaṅkāra), our thoughts and our desires. If we could only do all this while we are conscious, we could realise the Self.[64]

> Deep sleep is always present even in the waking state. What we have to do is to bring deep sleep into the waking state, to get "conscious sleep." Realization can only take place in the waking state. Deep sleep is relative to the waking state.[65]

This approach produces a surprising result. In an earlier discussion of the three states of consciousness — waking, dreaming and deep sleep the point was made that from the standpoint of Advaita two hierarchies seem to be involved here: William Indich labels them as subjective and objective. Using the criteria which serve to "distinguish the Self from phenomenal consciousness:"[66] (1) non-sublatability versus sublatability; (2) autonomy versus dependence; (3) certainty

63. Ann Faraday, *op. cit.*, p. 96.
64. Paul Brunton and Munagala Venkataramiah, *op. cit.*, p. 97.
65. *Ibid.*, p. 103.
66. William Indich, *op. cit.*, p. 54.

versus doubt and (4) non-duality versus duality; the three states of *phenomenal* consciousness were themselves arranged in the following hierarchy — waking, dreaming and deep sleep.[67] Their reconciliation is effected by suggesting that the subjective hierarchy points to the goal, and the objective hierarchy relates to the method to achieve the goal.[68]

What is being suggested here is that not only a *reconciliation but a synchronization* between the two hierarchies may be possible in the light of the dream-metaphor. If the subjective hierarchy indicates "the interiorization and unification of consciousness" as one moves from waking to dreaming to deep sleep states, then, in the context of objective hierarchy of method, following Ramaṇa, one raises waking-state-consciousness to dream (lucid dreaming) and to sleep (lucid sleep), thus leading to a similar upward movement both in terms of goal *and* method. The method also involves unification — or concentration and interiorization as unified waking consciousness penetrates upwards through other states. The point is further strengthened by a consideration of the concept of *pratyakṣa* or perception. *Pratyakṣa* or perception in the waking state involves the senses. In fact it "literally means *presented* to any sense."[69] In dream state, there are no senses operating as such and perception consists "in the direct and immediate presentation of an object to the mind."[70] In deep sleep, there is no perception as such — but what could be more thorough a "knowledge" than when the subject becomes identified with the object perceived! With this as the background one can feel the full force of Ramaṇa's remarks:

---

67. *Ibid.*, Chapter III.

68. *Ibid*, p. 65.

69. M. Hiriyanna, *Outlines of Indian Philosophy*, p. 345.

70. William Indich, *op. cit.*, p. 83.

Objects perceived by the senses are spoken of as immediate knowledge (*pratyakṣa*). Can anything be as direct as the Self — always experienced without the aid of the senses? Sense-perceptions can only be indirect knowledge, and not direct knowledge. Only one's own awareness is direct knowledge, as is the common experience of one and all. No aids are needed to know one's own Self, i.e., to be aware.[71]

71. *Talks with Śrī Ramaṇa Maharṣi*, p. 88.

9

The World as Dream and its Relation to Types of Dreams

A COMPARISON of the Advaitic analysis of dreaming, as one of the three states of consciousness, with modern speculations on the subject continues to be fruitful in the context of the metaphor of the world as dream. It is said that "six general analyses of the nature and origin of dreams were presented in classical [Hindu] thought" and that "Śaṅkara and his followers upheld, in one context or another, at least five of these six." This suggests that if ordinary dreams can be subjected to no less than six interpretations, the metaphor of the world as dream should certainly be capable of many interpretations — namely, that the world is subjective, or that our experience of it is mediated by mental content such as memory. For "research on the psychology of perception has shown that even an apparently simple observation has already been thoroughly processed in terms of our past experience and present preoccupations *before we even become aware of it*."[1] But perhaps one should first list the six analyses of dreams as identified by J. Sinha.[2] These may be called the presentative (that dreams merely present positive perceptions), the representative (that these perceptions are affected by memory and imagination), the hedonistic (my word: as pertaining to

1. Ann Faraday, *op. cit.*, p. 88.
2. J. Sinha, *op. cit.*, Chapter XV.

wish fulfilment), the retributive (involving karmic effects), the prophetic, the telepathic and the inclusive. This last requires a word of explanation, it "describes the phenomena known as 'dreams within dreams'" and "is categorized by Advaitins as a variety of representative type."[3] The world as dream as discussed hitherto seems to cover all of these, except the prophetic and the telepathic. If one includes the evidence from Ramaṇa, however, both of these are also accounted for. It is the last category, the inclusive, which now becomes particularly significant. This last type gains an independent status as a category as we move beyond "Śaṅkara and his followers" to Ramaṇa and his followers.

The literature on Ramaṇa contains a most curious example of a prophetic dream. On 18th February 1938:

> As Śrī Bhagavān was going through the letters which arrived this day, He read out one of them as follows:
>
> A Brāhmaṇa boy working in a household went to sleep as usual. In his sleep he cried out. When he woke up he said that he felt his prāṇa going out of the body through the mouth and nostrils. So he cried. Soon after he found himself dead and the soul taken to Vaikuṇṭha where God Viṣṇu was surrounded by other gods and devotees with prominent Vaishṇavite marks on their foreheads. Viṣṇu said, "This man should be brought here at 2 o'clock tomorrow. Why has he been brought here now?" The boy then woke up and related his experience. The next day at 2 o'clock he passed away.[4]

For a telepathic dream, or rather vision, one may cite the following phenomenon. I am not sure whether it entirely fits into the category but it will certainly serve to subliminally

---

3. William Indich, *op. cit.*, p. 88.
4. *Talks with Śrī Ramaṇa Maharṣi*, p. 435.

reactivate the reader's archetype about the inscrutable and mysterious East. It relates to the relationship between Ramaṇa and a well-known scholar, Gaṇapati Śāstrī[5] who is sometimes credited with having "discovered" Ramaṇa Maharṣi.

> In 1908 Śāstrī went away to Tiruvottiyur near Madras for *tapas*. There was a Gaṇeśa temple near which he performed his *tapas*, observing a vow of silence for eighteen days. On the eighteenth day, when he was lying wide awake, he saw the figure of Maharṣi coming in and sitting next to him. Sāstrī sat up in wonder and tried to get up. But Maharṣi pressed him down holding him by the head. This gave him something like an electric shock, which he regarded as *hastadīkṣa*, i.e., grace of the Guru conferred by a touch of his hand.
>
> Ever since Maharṣi arrived at Tiruvannāmalai on 1st September 1896 he had not left that place and never in his life had he seen Tiruvottiyur. But, as Sāstrī narrated the above in his presence on 17th October 1929, Maharṣi said:-
>
> One day some years ago I lay down, but I was not in samādhi. I suddenly felt my body carried up higher and higher till all objects disappeared and all around me was one vast mass of white light. Then suddenly the body descended and objects began to appear. I said to myself, "evidently this is how Siddhas appear and disappear." The idea occurred to me that I was at Tiruvottiyur. I was on a high road which went along. On one side and some distance removed from it was a Gaṇapati temple. I went in and talked, but what I said or did, I do not recollect. Suddenly I woke up and found myself lying in Virūpākṣa Cave. I mentioned this immediately to Palaniswāmī who was always with me.

---

5. *Ibid.*, pp. 301, 328, 376, 491, 518, 576-7.

> Śāstrī found that Maharṣi's description of the place at Tiruvottiyur exactly tallied with the Gaṇeśa temple in which he carried on his *tapas*.[6]

After this flight into regions unknown, one may now safely alight on the terra firma of academic investigation.

Some remarks made by Śaṅkara in the context of the presentative conception of dream seem capable of a promising extension in the context of the metaphor of the world as dream. Thus "Śaṅkara argues that although the *dream content*, e.g., seeing oneself flying through space is contradicted on waking, the *dream experience* itself remains an empirically real fact, i.e., one has actually dreamed that one flew through space."[7] It seems that the same could be said of the Realised one's experience of the world as dream. The world continues to constitute, as it were, a dream experience, but he or she knows the dream content to be false. This point would, of course, only apply when the world is seen by the Realised one, for "the experience of Consciousness can be with bodily awareness as well as without it."[8]

In the context of the representative conception of dream, "Śaṅkara asserts that the greater freedom demonstrated by consciousness in creating the objects and conditions of, and the emotional response to, its dream experience indicates that consciousness is actually more detached from its content in this state. Thus consciousness is not only involved in the creation of, but is also the witness to, dream experience."[9] At

---

6. B.V. Narasimha Swami, *Self-Realization: The Life and Teachings of Śrī Ramaṇa Maharṣi*, Tiruvannāmalai: Sri Ramanāsramam, 1985 pp. 94-95.
7. William Indich, *op. cit*, p. 84, emphasis added.
8. Arthur Osborne, ed., *op. cit.*, p. 192.
9. William Indich, *op. cit.*, p. 86.

its own empirical level this view finds an interesting parallel at the level of the waking state in the view that "anxiety is the enemy of creativity, and until it is removed, our minds will not be free to deal creatively with all the material that enters it during the waking state."[10] Could this greater detachment in dreams and relative freedom from anxiety account for the fact that sometimes breakthroughs have occurred in dreams? By pushing the same logic further one could suggest that even greater detachment is achieved in meditation, thus enabling spiritual breakthroughs to occur. However, once the world itself is treated as dream one immediately experiences this detachment "from the contents" even in the waking state.

The hedonistic view of dreams has also interesting implications for the metaphor of the world as dream. If one accepts Freud's idea in its starkest formulation, that *the motive of a dream is a wish and its content is the fulfilment of the wish*; or its Upaniṣadic counterpart: "He who desires, dreams; he who does not desire does not dream"[11] (*Bṛhadāraṇyaka Upaniṣad*: 4.3.19), then its applicability to the metaphor of the world as dream becomes quite striking in the Advaitic context. Liberation in Advaita is said to result from desirelessness. Thus the cessation of desires leads to the cessation of the world, or here the world-dream. There is a famous verse celebrating this, which is found both in the absolutistic Bṛhadāraṇyaka[12] and the theistic Kaṭha Upaniṣad:[13]

When all the desires that dwell in the heart are cast away,

---

10. Ann Faraday, *op. cit*, p. 294.

11. This is William Indich's translation; the original seems less direct though the sense is clear, see S. Radhakrishnan, ed., *The Principal Upaniṣads*, p. 261; Robert Ernest Hume, tr., *op. cit.*, p. 136.

12. IV.4.7.

13. VI.14.

> then does the mortal become immortal, then he attains Brahman here (in this very body).[14]

For Freud all wishes involved wish-fulfilment. Dreams are *frustrated* wishes and though the psychic residue of the subject contributes material to the dream, the dream-formation is only possible on account of the repressed wish. From the point of view of Advaita it will be fairer to say that (1) on the analogy of the psychic residue of a day with that of a life, rebirth is brought about by repressed wish-impulses *in* the "residue of the previous day" and (2) that not merely repressed but manifest wishes are equally involved in the process of rebirth. These points are important because they have a bearing on the answers one finds to the obvious question: if dreams involve wish-fulfilment, then why are they sometimes painful? The fact of wishes being repressed wishes will go a long way towards providing an answer in the case of Freud. In the case of Advaita the answer would be philosophically more complex, especially in the context of the metaphor of the world as dream. To take just one instance, one may wish but not understand fully the implication of one's wish. Hence the distilled wisdom of the saying that more tears have been shed over answered prayers than over unanswered ones and the Shavian warning to be careful about what one wants, lest one get it. The predicament is suitably illustrated by the following anecdote:

> There was a poor man who had heard that if he got hold of a ghost he could get what he wanted. He came to a sage reputed to have great powers. The sage asked him, "What would you do with the ghost?" The poor man said, "I want the ghost to work under my command, for I desire so many things." The sage told him that he could not help him. The man, however, again went up to him the next day and began

14. S. Radhakrishnan, ed., p. 273.

to weep saying that he must have a ghost. At last the sage, in order to get rid of him, gave him a magic word and said that if the word was repeated the ghost would come and do his bidding. He, however, told the poor man to see that the ghost was kept fully busy; otherwise the ghost would take his life. Having received the advice, the man went into a forest and uttered the magic word repeatedly whereupon the ghost made its appearance before him and said, "I have appeared by the force of your magic word. Give me some employment; otherwise I shall kill you." "Build me a palace," said the man and immediately he saw a beautiful palace standing before his eyes. The man next said, "Bring me large quantities of money." And the next moment large piles of gold and silver coins were lying at his feet. The man next ordered the ghost to cut down the forest and build a city in its place. The transformation took place in the twinkling of an eye and then the ghost demanded "What shall I do now?" The man was at a loss to think of any fresh orders and this made him frightened, feeling that the ghost was going to kill him. The ghost also told him, "Give me something to do or I shall kill you." Thereupon the poor man began to run to the place where the sage who had given him the charm was sitting. "Oh sir, protect my life," implored the man and as he was explaining what had happened the ghost arrived saying, "I shall now eat you up," and it was on the point of swallowing the man. The sage said to the man, "You just draw your sword and cut the tail of the dog which is standing there. Give the tail to the ghost and ask him to straighten it out." The man cut the dog's tail and giving it to the ghost said, "Now straighten this out for me." When the ghost straightened the tail and let it go, it immediately curled up again. Again and again the ghost straightened it out only to find that it curled up as soon as the ghost let go of it. This went on for days and days until the ghost out of sheer despair said, "I have never been in such a trouble before." Going up to the man it said, "Will

> you let me off? If you will let me go I promise I will never harm you." The man agreed and the ghost disappeared forever.[15]

The case of telepathic and prophetic dreams has already been covered. The category of dream-within-dreams has not been as clearly explicated as seems desirable, if it is to provide a fresh perspective on the metaphor of the world as dream.[16] The category is quite germane to the present discussion if one follows the *Yogavāsiṣṭha* deep into the following cosmic landscape:

> The terms cosmic Mind and individual mind are, according to Vasiṣṭha, relative. That which is an individual in relation to a wider and more comprehensive cosmic Mind and its contents, may, in its own turn, be considered to be cosmic in relation to the entities (ideas) within its own objective experience. For, according to him, every object has a subjective aspect, i.e., in a mind, in which is experienced a world peculiar to itself, as in a dream. Every idea, thus, is a monad in itself and has a world within its experience, every ideal content of which is, again, in its turn, in itself, an individual monad having another within itself. There is no end to this process of worlds within worlds. In this way, in each universe are contained millions of other universes, and this process goes on ad infinitum. All this is unknown and unreal to us, but is directly known to those who have attained perfection.[17]

Two points arise for clarification in the context of dreams-within-dreams: whether dreams within dreams are presentative or representative and whether the "new" dream

15. Swami Sambuddhānanda, *op. cit.*, pp. 73-75.
16. Jadunath Sinha, *op. cit.*, vol I, pp. 321-22.
17. B.L. Atreya, *op. cit.*, p. 426. For the full text of the work involved see Vihari Lal Mitra, *The Yoga-Vāsiṣṭha of Vālmīki*, Delhi: Parimal Publications, 1998.

is a new dream within the old dream, that is "subjective"; or is it an old dream within the new dream — that is "objective." In other words, is one dream experienced fresh by the subject in another dream; or is a dream the object of another dream. If all these possibilities are granted then the more representative a dream-in-dream is and the more objective it is, the more Karmically encumbered it is going to be.

The sixfold classification of dreams in Hindu psychology, as adopted by Advaita, is interesting in itself. Some interesting variations of the metaphorical theme become possible when this classification is applied to the metaphor of the world as dream and each item in the classification of dreams is brought into connection with the understanding of the *antaḥkaraṇa* or the "inner organ" as found in Advaita, or with a combination of the functions ascribed to it.[18] The following comment of Śaṅkara is helpful in explicating the concept of *antaḥkaraṇa* or the internal organ: "The internal organ which constitutes the limiting adjunct of the soul is called in different places by different names, such as *manas* (mind), *buddhi* (intelligence), *vijñāna* (knowledge), *citta* (thought) and *ahaṅkāra* (egoism). This difference of nomenclature is something made dependent on the difference of the modifications of the internal organ which is called *manas* when it is in the state of doubt, etc. *buddhi* when it is in the state of determination and the like."[19] Sometimes these names are taken as more clearly indicative of its functions: thus *manas* is associated with perception; *buddhi* with the discriminative faculty; *vijñāna* with knowledge of all kinds; *citta* with memory and *ahaṅkāra* with egoism.[20] This

18. William Indich, *op. cit.*, p. 86, begins to move his discussion in this direction but then seems to stop short.

19. Eliot Deutsch and J.A.B. van Buitenen, *op. cit.*, p. 193.

20. Surendranath Dasgupta, *A History of Indian Philosophy*, Cambridge: Cambridge University Press, 1951, vol. I, p. 460.

multiple identification of *antaḥkaraṇa* as (1) sense-mind (*manas*); (2) memory (*citta*); (3) discriminative faculty (*buddhi*); (4) egoism (*ahaṅkāra*) and (5) knowledge (*vijñāna*) enables the frontiers of suggestion to be pushed further, for now each of these aspects of *antaḥkaraṇa* can be associated with one formulation of the sixfold theory of dreams. The presentative theory links up with *manas* and the representative with *citta*. Although William Indich associates wish-fulfilment with *buddhi*, some might feel happier associating it with *ahaṅkāra* or the ego in search of gratification. Prophetic dreams could be associated with *vijñāna*, and the telepathic with *alaukikavijñāna* or paranormal knowledge. If one accepts the view that dreams-within-dreams belong to the category of representative dreams, then *buddhi* as a function of the mind is left out without a counterpart. Perhaps it will answer to the category of lucid dreams. Indeed the comparison between the Indian classification of dreams with the Western generates quite a few fruitful points of interest. It is possible to suggest, for instance, that Freud's theory of wish-fulfilment about dreams is a combination of *citta* plus *kalpanā* (imagination) which characterizes the representative category of Hindu dreams, with the element of *buddhi* (or the discrimination of *dharma* and *adharma*) having infiltrated *citta*.[21] Similarly, on the level of the metaphor of the *world* as dream, the role of *buddhi*, with its etymological connection to the root *budh*, to awaken, should not be overlooked.

The discussion hitherto has surveyed the cases of individual dream but what about the collective dimension? Jung introduces it in the concept of the collective unconscious and the *Yogavāsiṣṭha* speaks of the universe as the dream of Brahmā. Brahmā is portrayed in some texts, as for instance, in

---

21. William Indich, *op. cit.*, p. 90.

the *Manusmṛti*,[22] as the promulgator of the institutes of *varṇa*. If *varṇa* and *āśrama* (or classes of human beings and stages of human life), are part and parcel of the divine dream, could it be suggested that *varṇa* and *āśrama* in a way represent Jungian archetypes — with the persistent tendency of humanity to divide itself up into classes and of life to ritually negotiate the transitional points in the continuum of life? Thus while it is true that in Advaita "the goal of human life entails transcendence of the stages of life" it could nevertheless be true that for both the Advaitin in the world as well as the Jungian subject, the collective "dream" or "unconscious" "functions teleogically in striving to present its wisdom, concerning the progressive stages of human experience, to man at the appropriate transitions in life when this wisdom can serve to guide him towards his potential perfection or individuation, i.e., creative and whole living in the world."[23]

> Jung also provides some other interesting points of comparison and contrast in relation to Advaita. Two of these are readily identified. Firstly, "Śaṅkara maintains that the general condition of the individual's sub-conscious impressions parallels the moral quality of the individual's waking activity and experience . . . this position is exactly opposite to what Jung calls the compensatory function of the unconscious as it manifests in dreams."[24] For Jung is arguing that the psyche as a whole is a "self-regulating system" and that the success of its regulatory activity

22. *Manusmṛti* I.31.87.
23. William Indich, *op. cit.*, p. 94. That Advaita is not unconcerned with the realm, though it aspires to transcend it, is also brought home by the parallel between prophetic dreams in Advaita and what Jung calls the "prospective" function of dreams (*ibid.*, p. 94 note 4).
24. *Ibid.*, p. 87.

> requires the collective unconscious to oppose conscious content and thereby to guide man to increased self-realization. And the place where this opposition is most evident, he concludes, is in our dreams. For this reason Jung claims that the dream content, which reveals its meaning directly and non-deceptively, complements rather than parallels the content of waking experience. . . . He refers to this complementary opposition as the "compensatory relationship" between the unconscious and conscious layers of the psyche.[25]

The contrast between the Advaitin and Jungian views of dreams however diminishes when applied to the metaphor of the world as dream. For then the opposition between *saṁsāra* and *mokṣa,* at the soteriological level, provides a parallel to the opposition between the individual and collective unconscious.

Nevertheless it cannot be denied that the gulf between the two realms — the psychological realm of Jung and the metaphysical realm to which the Advaitic metaphor of the world as dream applies, cannot be bridged. This emerges clearly from the goals of the two systems — individuation in Jung and Atmanization in Advaita. Although a clear empirical self-definition is required before one can proceed on the Advaitic path, this constitutes a *preparation* not the goal of the path. And while individuation is the goal of the Jungian path, the goal of the Advaitin's path, if anything, is de-individuation in the sense of the dissolution of the sense of individuality, or ego or "I"-ness. Some might even find the consummation alarming that after the inquiry "Who am I?" is relentlessly pursued in Advaita as advocated by Ramaṇa,[26]

---

25. *Ibid.*, p. 94.

26. Although modern Advaitins are to be credited with giving →

> The true answer to the question Who am I does not come in thoughts. All thoughts disappear — even the thinker himself disappears.[27]
>
> *Ātman* is *Brahman* after all!

This brings us to the consideration of the limitations of the comparative approach, in the course of pursuing which we not only compared Advaitic theories of dreams with modern theories but also compared them both with the metaphor of the world as dream as well. One interesting limitation is suggested by Śaṅkara's comment about ordinary dreams that presumably in the case of most "a dream is not an entirely new experience, for most often it is the memory of past experiences."[28] If we transfer this idea to the metaphor of the world as dream then its implication would seem to be that the universe, and we in the universe, repeatedly re-experience past experiences. Or to put it more simply — repeat our experiences. It has even been suggested that the universe is repeatedly undergoing identical or at least similar cycles,[29] though no one seems to have wondered if this cosmic cloning leads to replicative degeneration, as with photocopying. There is a hint in Ramaṇa along the same lines when he cites the Ṛgvedic text: "*Dhātā yathā-pūrvam akalpayat* (the creator created

---

→ centrality to the mode of self-inquiry epitomized by a koan-like grappling with the question: who am I? the procedure is not entirely novel. It is alluded to in both the Mārkaṇḍeya and the Viṣṇu Purāṇa; see F. Eden Pargiter, tr., *The Mārkaṇḍeya Purāṇa*, Delhi: Indological Book House, 1969, p. 215; and *Viṣṇu Purāṇa*, Book II, Chapter 15-16.

27. Paul Brunton and Munagala Venkataramiah, *op. cit.*, p. 169.

28. William Indich, *op. cit.*, p. 85.

29. Heinrich Zimmer, *Myths and Symbols in Indian Art and Civilization*, p. 18.

just as before)."[30] But it is not at all clear if such is indisputably the case. The Ṛgvedic text itself provides an interesting example. M. Hiriyanna states that in the *Ṛgveda* "When the universe is spoken of as creation, only one creation is mentioned; and the belief, so well known to a later age, in a series of creations, each being followed by a dissolution is absent."[31] At this point he observes in a footnote "There seems to be a stray reference to it in RV. X.190.3: *dhātā yathā-pūrvam akalpayat*. But it may be interpreted differently." He alludes here to Deussen's explanation that the expression may mean successively — one after the other.[32] Thus first of all whether there is a cyclic process, at least at this stage in the history of Hinduism, is in doubt. It is no doubt in place by the time of Śaṅkara, but already it is being questioned if each aeon is alike. The different accounts of the birth of Gaṇeśa, for instance, are reconciled by suggesting that he is born differently in different ages.[33] It could however be argued that even this may be part of a more gargantuan and diversified repetitive cyclical scheme. In any case, Śaṅkara would seem to favour a cyclical notion, perhaps one rigidly so.[34] The real problem here is not historical but philosophical. Once it is conceded that the world is like a dream and a product of the mind which is changeable, would the universe not be likewise? Maybe it is not amenable to whim but surely to an act of creative will as later Advaita affirms in citing the story of Viśvāmitra. "Viśvāmitra, a great *ṛṣi*, is reputed to have created a duplicate

30. *Talks with Śrī Ramaṇa Maharṣi*, pp. 106-07.

31. M. Hiriyanna, *Outlines of Indian Philosophy*, p. 44.

32. *Ibid.*, p. 44 note 4.

33. T.M.P. Mahadevan, *Outlines of Hinduism*, Bombay: Chetana Limited, 1971, p. 183.

34. K. Satchidananda Murty, *Revelation and Reason in Advaita Vedānta*, Delhi: Motilal Banarsidass, 1974, p. 40.

Universe, a part of which consists of the constellations composing Scorpio, Sagittarius, and the Southern Cross. Some trees, plants and herbs in imitation of well-known species (e.g., palmyra corresponding to coconut, jungle potatoes and onions insipid to taste and useless, etc.) are among his creations."[35]

The situation gets complicated if one introduces another element from Śaṅkara's analysis of dreams, namely, of *dharma* and *adharma*, or of good and bad deeds.[36] If the new universe comes into being with a retributive end in mind — namely, to provide the *jīva*s with the results of their *karma*, then it must be remoulded in the light of their *karma* unless their *karma* is totally and eternally predestined. In this case then how is *karma* in Hinduism different from the *niyati* of Makkhali Gosāla?[37]

Thus Śaṅkara's *empirical* analysis of dream has serious limitations when applied to the *metaphorical* analysis of the world as dream.

Śaṅkara also uses the dream experience to establish the proof of *ātman*.

> Śaṅkara argues that the fact that consciousness witnesses its dreams means that consciousness reveals or illumines them. Indeed, without the aid of the external senses and physical light, what other than the light of consciousness itself illumines dream objects? In other words, beginning with the creativity and detachment of dream consciousness from its content, Śaṅkara argues both for the continuity of self-awareness throughout the various states of experience as well as for the self-luminosity of consciousness itself. In

---

35. Swami Sri Ramanananda Saraswathi, tr., *op. cit.*, p. 86, also see 91.
36. William Indich, *op. cit.*, p. 87.
37. Wm. Theodore de Bary et, al., *Sources of Indian Tradition*, p. 42.

> this way Śaṅkara attaches great metaphysical significance to the analysis of dream experience in general, and to the point that dream objects are the creation of the mind in particular. Indeed, he says that "By the illustration of dreams it has been proved that there is the self-luminous *ātman* and that it transcends the forms of death [i.e., is eternal.]"[38]

It is difficult to be convinced entirely by such metaphysical extrapolation in the context of the world as dream. Some arguments seem doubtless persuasive — especially the one which pertains to the emergence of an apparently objective world out of the subject. And it could be argued that dream implies a dreamer, *outside* the dream. But this is where the analogy seems to falter, for the dream could as well be a creation of those within the dream, not outside it, at the cosmic level, like Brahmā being part of Viṣṇu's dream. One could argue for a *sākṣī* on the basis of an experiencer of the three discontinuous and therefore autonomous states of consciousness — of waking, dream and deep sleep but it is not clear if the argument using the dream state *alone* could be that cogent.

The third point of limitation emerges from evidence which is admittedly anecdotal and biographical but nevertheless relevant. I repeat the account as I received it from my mother. At some stage in his career, when my father was facing professional obstacles of a serious nature, my mother consulted a local for advice. He gave her a *mantra* to repeat, but warned her that its use will result in nightmares, which will be proof that it is having effect. Soon enough (perhaps because of the suggestion itself?) my mother started having such horrifying

38. William Indich, *op. cit.*, p. 86.

nightmares that she discontinued repeating the *mantra*, although my father's situation did seem to improve. After the interval of some years she became a follower of Swāmī Chinmayānanda, who went on to become a fairly well-known Advaitin Swami in India and abroad. This is how he explained the phenomenon to my mother: my mother was destined to work out some bad *karma* through the difficulties my father was facing. All the *mantra* did was to transfer the experience from the waking to the dreaming state. It had to be experienced — in some form or other. Whether it was experienced in the waking state or the dreaming state was ultimately inconsequential.

This transfer of *karma* from one state of consciousness to another was news to me. One has, of course, heard of transfer of *karma* from one person to another and this is still possible on the metaphor of the world as dream. But if the "waking state" itself is placed on a par with dream, where could then such *karma* be transferred? To a dream within a dream? Or from one dream to another?

10

The Dream Metaphor
Some Problems

THE dream-metaphor is not without its problems, despite its illustrative convenience in an Advaitic context.

A major difficulty in employing the dream-metaphor in Advaita lies in this — that it tends to make the Advaitic position similar to the subjectivism of the *vijñānavāda*, which it is eager to refute. As the dreams emerge from and merge into a dreamer, the metaphor is suggestive of subjective idealism, as also the fact that the contents of dream consciousness may be capable of being explained in terms of subjective experience. Śaṅkara however attacks subjective idealism. As Eliot Deutsch notes regarding Śaṅkara's comment on *Brahma-Sūtra* II.2.28:

> Śaṅkara's attack on subjective idealism is, in this conext, directed against the *vijñānavāda* school of Buddhism which did uphold the position that the contents of empirical consciousness could be accounted for entirely in terms of the activities of consciousness alone. The realism of Advaita is in opposition to this position both on theoretical and practical grounds. It is argued theoretically that subject/object experience means precisely a distinction between subject and object, which distinction can be overcome only through transcendence; and practically that any doctrine of subjectivism becomes a barrier to this act of transcendence.[1]

---

1. Eliot Deutsch, *op.cit.*, p. 31 fn. 8.

He goes on to add: "In later Vedānta, however, a kind of subjectivism called *dṛṣṭi-sṛṣṭi-vāda* ("doctrine that perception is creation") was put forward (by Prakāśānanda), but it was argued for in a somewhat different philosophical context, and, in any event, it would clearly have been rejected by Śaṅkara and his early followers. (Cf. Appaya Diksitar, *Siddhāntaleśasaṁgraha*, 3:711.)"[2] The second point to note is Śaṅkara's position in general:

> For Advaita Vedānta, then, the phenomenal world is *māyā*, and it is produced by *māyā*. But it is not on that account merely a figment of one's imagination. With the possible exception of Prakāśānanda, Advaitic thinkers hold that a subjective idealism is not the proper philosophical expression or consequence of a doctrine of *māyā*. So far as a separate subject exists, so does the object that is experienced by it. Duality is transcended only in an experience that is different in kind from what takes place in the subject/object situation.[3]

A third point worth noting is that Western scholarship has tended to ignore this fine point. Eliot Deutsch observes for instance:

> It is rather curious that this aspect of classical Advaita has been overlooked frequently by Western students of Indian thought. In our rush to read Vedānta as an extension of either the Hegelian or Berkeleyan idealistic traditions, we fail to appreciate its distinctive character. For Advaita, "oneness" holds only on the level of Brahman-experience and must never be confounded with the world of multiplicity (the world of *nāma-rūpa* — names and forms). Any confusion between the two is precisely the basic characteristic of that

2. *Ibid*.
3. *Ibid*., p. 31.

> false superimposition (*adhyāsa*), which is ignorance (*avidyā*).[4]

Indian scholars, on the other hand, regularly refer to this point.[5] The general position of Śaṅkara on this point may be summarized thus:

> . . . he asserts that the objects of normal waking experience are not on a par with dream-objects, since dream-experience is contradicted by waking experience, which, therefore, is relatively more real; that external objects, like pillars, pots, etc. which are immediately felt to be outside the mind cannot be reduced to the status of mere ideas in the mind, and that while the former are perceived by all the latter only by the individual in whose mind they are. He also makes it clear that though he explains the world on the analogy of a dream he does not deny the difference between the contradicted dream-experience and the contradicting waking experience on which the world is based, nor does he overlook the fact that these two experiences are differently caused. The ignorance responsible for the first is of an individual and temporary nature, and that at the root of the second is general and relatively permanent. The first is sometimes called *avidyā* (individual ignorance), the second *māyā* (general ignorance), though these two terms are also sometimes used synonymously in the sense of illusion-producing ignorance in general.[6]

It must, however, also be pointed out that the dream-metaphor *if properly understood on its own terms* can correctly reflect Śaṅkara's position in particular and the Advaitic position in general. To see this one should visualize the dream

4. *Ibid.*, pp. 94-95.
5. M. Hiriyanna, *Outlines of Indian Philosophy*, p. 367.
6. Satischandra Chatterjee and Dhirendramohas Datta, *op. cit.*, pp. 393-94.

being preceded by a state of deep sleep which is devoid of the subject-object division and an empirical reminder of the possibility of undifferentiated consciousness. Then out of it the dream emerges, like the universe from Brahman. The dream world too, like the real world, bifurcates into dream subject or subjects and objects.

Another major difficulty is presented by the role of responsibility in relation to the world as dream. Actions performed by us in ordinary dreams do not entail karmic responsibility, but actions committed in the world do. Several considerations need to be taken into account here. On account of the close association of sleeping and dreaming, one could be absolved of all responsibility for one's actions on the basis of the dream-metaphor. According to the Buddhists, for instance, "in a dream the monk is absolved from sins committed in dreams."[7] Rajneesh may or may not have been influenced by this view when he says:

> So from the initiated it is a surrendering of the past. From the one who initiates you, it is a responsibility for the future. He becomes responsible, and only he can be responsible. You can never be responsible. How can one who is asleep be responsible? Responsibility is never a part of sleep. If you commit a murder in your sleep, it you are a somnambulist walking in your sleep and you commit a murder, no court will make you responsible, because there is no responsibility.
>
> A person who is in deep sleep, how is he responsible? You never feel responsible for your dreams. You may murder, but you say that it was just a dream. Responsibility comes with awakening. This is really a fundamental law of life.

---

7. P.T. Raju, "Indian Philosophy" in Haridas Bhattacharyya, ed., *op. cit.*, Volume III, p. 598.

> One who is asleep is not responsible even for himself, and one who is awakened is responsible even for others.
>
> A person who is Enlightened, who is awakened, feels he is even responsible for the whole mess that you have created. A Buddha feels compassion. Buddha feels guilty for your crimes, for your sins. He feels involved; he feels responsible. He knows that you do not know; he is fully aware.[8]

However even Rajneesh maintains the view that the Guru works with the disciples' dreams.[9] A much more direct statement on this point comes from Ramaṇa.

> From the point of view of *jñāna* (knowledge) or the reality, the pain seen in the world is certainly a dream as is the world of which any particular pain like hunger you refer to is an infinitesimal part. In the dream also you yourself feel hunger. You see others suffering from hunger. You feed yourself, and moved by pity feed the others whom you find suffering from hunger. So long as the dream lasted all those pains were quite as real as you now think the pain in the world to be. It was only when you woke up that you discovered that the pain in the dream was unreal. You might have eaten to the full and gone to sleep. You dream that you work hard and long in the hot sun all day, are tired and find your stomach is full and you have not stirred out of your bed. But all this is not to say that while you are in the dream you can act as if the pain you feel there is not real. The hunger in the dream has to be assuaged by the food in the dream. The fellow being you found so hungry in the dream had to be provided with food in that dream. You can never mix up the two states, the dream and the waking state. Till you reach the state of *jñāna* and thus wake out of *māyā* you must do social service by relieving suffering whenever you

---

8. Bhagwan Shree Rajneesh, *I am the Gate*, Bombay (Mumbai): Life Awakening Center, 1972, p. 162.
9. *Ibid.*, p. 179.

> see it. But even then you must do it without *ahaṁkāra,* i.e., without the sense of "I am the doer," but feeling "I am the Lord's tool." Similarly one must not be conceited "I am helping a man below me. He needs help. I am in a position to help. I am superior and he inferior," but you must help the man as a means of worshipping God in that man. All such service too is for the Self and not for anybody else. You are not helping anybody else, but only yourself.[10]

It is significant that in this context he connects the state of non-discrimination between right and wrong not with the state of dream but that of deep sleep.[11]

A third difficulty may also be identified. Inasmuch as the idea of the unreality of the world has been associated with Advaita, though erroneously, it is said to suggest as attitude of total irresponsibility. Eliot Deutsch, along with a host of scholars, points out that in Advaita the world far from being unreal "is distinguished from true reality (*sat*) and from complete non-reality (*asat*)."[12] He goes on to say:

> It is necessary to emphasize this rather strongly because Advaita Vedānta has so often been presented to the West as

10. David Godman, ed., *op. cit.*, p. 212.
11. Swami Rajeswarananda, *Erase the Ego,* Bombay (Mumbai): Bharatiya Vidya Bhavan, 1974, p. 35: "To see wrong in another is one's own wrong projected. The discrimination between right and wrong is the origin of the sin. One's own sin is reflected outside and the individual in ignorance superimposes it on another. The best course is to reach the state in which such discrimination does not arise. Do you see wrong or right in your sleep? Be asleep even in the wakeful state, abide as the Self and remain uncontaminated by what goes on around. Your silence will have more effect than your words and deeds. That is the development of will-power. Then the world becomes the Kingdom of Heaven, which is within you."
12. Eliot Deutsch, *op. cit.*, p. 32.

> a philosophy that simply condemns the world to unreality. For Advaita, the world, from the standpoint of reason or subject/object consciousness, is neither real nor unreal (as these terms have been defined): the world is an illusion only on the basis of an experience of the Absolute. The world cannot be an illusion to one who lacks that experience. Empirical reality, in other words, is transcended only absolutely. Only from the viewpoint of the infinite does everything but itself appear as without substance, without independent reality and value. In short: "*there is no reason to call the world unreal before the knowledge of the oneness of the Ātman (has been attained)*." (Sureśvara, Sambandha Vārttika, as quoted by N.K. Devaraja in *An Introduction to Śaṅkara's Theory of Knowledge* (Delhi: Motilal Banarsidas, 1962) p. 16.[13]

This limitation points to yet another. If dream is non-volitional, and life is like a dream, then no volition can be exercised in dreams — even for awakening from it! The non-volitional character of dreams stands out dramatically in their characterization by C.G. Jung. Even those who do not agree with the content of his psychology will probably accept his emphasis on their involuntary character, irrespective of speculations about their origin:

> When a situation occurs which corresponds to a given archetype, that archetype becomes activated and a compulsiveness appears, which, like an instinctual drive, gains its way against all reason and will, or else produces a conflict of pathological dimensions, that is to say, a neurosis.
>
> ----
>
> We must now turn to the question of how the existence of archetypes can be proved. Since archetypes are supposed to produce certain psychic forms, we must discuss how and where one can get hold of the material demonstrating

13. Eliot Deutsch and J.A.B. van Buitenen, *op. cit.*, p. 193.

> these forms. *The main source, then, is dreams, which have the advantage of being involuntary, spontaneous products of the unconscious psyche and are therefore pure products of nature not falsified by any conscious purpose.* By questioning the individual one can ascertain which of the motifs appearing in the dream are known to him.[14]

The dream-metaphor in effect tends to undermine the role of *Īśvara* in the Advaitic scheme. From another point of view it may even seem to undermine the role of the *jīva*. For, in order to visualize the world as dream one needs the dream and that which contains it. Thus Brahman and *māyā* suffice to explain the universe — the category of *Īśvara* who is not deluded by *māyā* and the *jīva*s who are, are both subsequent to *māyā*. The *jīva*s could be looked upon as a product of *māyā* and one may not need to posit an overlord of the dream. Hence the dream-metaphor, by itself, tends to marginalize two categories which play an important role in Advaita. Advaitic thought, however, utilizes the dream-metaphor in such a way as to accommodate these features of it. Thus *Īśvara* is looked upon as the Dreamer and the *Jīva* is part of the dream. This is how *Īśvara* and *Jīva* are accommodated in the version of creation known as *sṛṣṭi-dṛṣṭi-vāda*.[15]

How the *sṛṣṭi-dṛṣṭi-vāda* was cast by M. Hiriyanna[16] in the dream-metaphor has already been indicated. The other two doctrines of *ajātavāda* and *dṛṣṭi-sṛṣṭi-vāda*, discussed earlier, as cast by Ramaṇa in the same metaphor was demonstrated earlier. The passage is cited below for the sake of convenience.

> The question arises why then do all the *śāstra*s speak of the Lord as the creator? How can the creature, that you are,

---

14. Surendranath Dasgupta, *op. cit.*, p. 460.
15. David Godman, ed., *op. cit.*, p. 184.
16. M. Hiriyanna, *Outlines of Indian Philosophy*, p. 367.

> create the creator and argue that the *jagat, jīva* and *Īśvara* are mental conceptions only?
>
> The answer is as follows:-
>
> You know that your father of this *jāgrat* state is dead and that several years have elapsed since his death. However you see him in your dream and recognize him to be your father, of whom you were born and who has left patrimony to you. Here the creator is in the creature. Again, you dream that you are serving a king and that you are a part in the administrative wheel of the kingdom. As soon as you wake up all of them have disappeared leaving you, the single individual, behind. Where were they all? Only in yourself. The same analogy holds good in the other case also.[17]

Herein the example of the first dream served to illustrate *dṛṣṭi-sṛṣṭi-vāda* and of the second *ajātavāda.*

A fourth difficulty presented by the dream-metaphor is caused by the conflation of a direct physical distinction (with all its metaphysical resonance) between the two, sleep and waking, wherein dream is subsumed in sleep, and the physiological distinction between the *three* states of waking, dreaming and deep sleep.

The telescoping of the trichotomy into the dichtomy is almost a regular feature in some forms of Advaita. Thus Gauḍapāda, for instance, after discussing the empirical differences between them maintains that, despite the empirical differences, "from the metaphysical point of view both are the same. The states of dream and waking are the one, say the wise."[18] And when Ramaṇa was asked: "Is there any real distinction between dream and waking?" he answered: "Only

---

17. *Talks with Śrī Ramaṇa Maharṣi,* p. 374. The passage was also cited earlier.
18. T.M.P. Mahadevan, *Gauḍapāda: A Study in Early Advaita,* p. 126.

apparent not real. The dream is for one who says that he is awake. Both are unreal from the absolute viewpoint."[19]

In order to comprehend the situation one must move in three steps. As a first step, there is only a twofold distinction between Sleeping and Awakening; between sleep and Realization. From this point of view:

> One is always in sleep only. The present waking state is no more than a dream. Dream can take place only in sleep. Sleep is underlying these three states. The display as those three states is again a dream which is in its turn, in another sleep. In this way, these states of dream and sleep are endless.[20]

It is difficult to grasp the latter half of the citation as it sends one's mind careening through a vertiginous spiral without a finite opening but the early half of the sentence is plain enough. The same point is clarified elsewhere by Ramaṇa thus:

> What happens to the consciousness of a Realised one in sleep? Such a question arises only in the minds of unrealised beholders. He has but One state, which is unbroken throughout the 24 hours, whether in what you call sleeping or waking. As a matter of fact the majority of people are all asleep, because they are not awake to the Self.[21]

The second half of the original statement which was meant to be explained in part by what has just been cited, is to be understood in the following frame of reference. If we correlate the three states of consciousness as commonly understood and the metaphysical sleep and dream, we shall find that in the state of waking there are both dream and sleep, viz.

---

19. Paul Brunton and Munagala Venkataramiah, *op. cit.*, p. 101.
20. Paul Brunton and Munagala Venkataramiah, *op. cit.*, p. 98.
21. *Ibid.*, p. 96.

misapprehension and non-apprehension of the real, in the state of dream there is sleep also, and in the state of sleep there is sleep alone. The metaphysical sleep continues throughout transmigratory life. Its spell is broken only at the onset of knowledge.[22]

It is the juxtaposition of the physical trichotomy, the metaphysical dichotomy and the transcendental monotony which creates difficulties.

Thus, as a first step, one recognizes a dichotomy between Waking and Sleep wherein Waking corresponds to Realization and Sleep to non-Realization.

One must next descend a step down the ladder to explore only Sleep or our world of mundane existence, ignoring for the time being the transcendental realm of Awakening. Now here again one encounters another dichotomy: deep sleep and dreaming. In the realm of deep sleep one nests as closely as one can to the transcendental realm, veiled by *avidyā* or nescience in its primal form.[23] The dichotomy here is between deep (i.e., dreamless sleep) and dreaming, between sleep and dream as it were, because *essentially* there is no difference between what we call the "waking state" and the "dreaming state." Upon examination, Ramaṇa points out, "You will find the world of which you are now aware is just as unreal as the world in which you lived in your dream."[24]

Now one may descend down the ladder further and arrive at another dichotomy — that of "dreaming" between the "dream state" and the "waking state."

Thus the following pattern emerges:

---

22. T.M.P. Mahadevan, *Gauḍapāda: A Study in Early Advaita*, p. 105.
23. M. Hiriyanna, *Outlines of Indian Philosophy*, p. 348.
24. David Godman, ed., *op. cit.*, p. 189.

Awakening (general state of Realization)
Sleeping (general state of non-realization)
Sleeping — deep sleep in general
Dreaming — particular dream state
Particular waking state

Some of the difficulties in understanding Advaita arise from the dual use of waking and sleeping; the dual use of sleep and the dual use of dreaming. The standard Advaitic formulation has just four levels:

awakening	(*turīya*)
deep sleep	(*suṣupti*)
dream state	(*svapna*)
waking state	(*jāgrat*)

Would it help if sleeping in general were called *nidrā*, awakening, *prabodha*, and dreaming in general *svapnavṛtti* in contrast to *svapnāvasthā*? Such fine distinctions have often been attempted[25] but the tetrachotomy has stood the test of time. As Ramaṇa explained in a passage cited earlier:

> There is no difference between dream and the waking state except that the dream is short and the waking long. Both are the result of the mind. Because the waking state is long, we imagine that it is our real state. But, as a matter of fact, our real state is *turīya* or the fourth state which is always as it is and knows nothing of the three states of waking, dream or sleep. Because we call these three *avasthā*s [states] we call the fourth state also *turīya avasthā*. But it is not an *avasthā*, but the real and natural state of the Self. When this is realised, we know it is not a *turīya* or fourth state, for a fourth state is only relative, but *turīyatīta*, the transcendent state.[26]

25. T.M.P. Mahadevan, *Gauḍapāda: A Study in Early Advaita*, pp. 107-08.
26. David Godman, ed., *op. cit.*, p. 16. Also see p. 15. This passage has been cited earlier.

This tetrachotomy may be the neatest, perhaps even the best but is only near-perfect, as is apparent from attempts to label dreams in different ways. When Ramaṇa admits that the Realised being "does dream" he adds as noted earlier, "but he knows it to be a dream, in the same way as he knows the waking state to be a dream. You may call them dream no. 1 and dream no. 2."[27] The *Tripurā-Rahasya* speaks of "a dream in a dream" which is explained by the commentator as when "a dreamer mistakes a dream-rope in a dream-serpent (the dream is itself an illusion and the mistake is an illusion in an illusion)."[28] One may also consider the following possibility: that "dreams within dreams are recollections of dream-cognitions."[29]

A fifth difficulty presented by the dream-metaphor relates to the problem of multiple dreams. The attempt to resolve this has often been suspected as leading to solipsism, a tendency the reader would have certainly recognized by now and may have even identified as a problem. What seems like a logical development has also to some extent been a historical development. This would seem to be the cul-de-sac, as one races down the road of the dream-metaphor. The problem of "objective criteria" of the world can only be fully resolved, on one view, by its increasing subjectivization so that in the end no one is left apart from the dreamer to question it. For idealism takes the position that "Just as in cases of dreams and hallucinations a man fancies to perceive things outside, though they really do not exist there, similarly the objects

27. *Ibid.*, p. 37.

28. Swami Sri Ramaṇānanda Saraswathi, tr., *op. cit.*, p. 98.

29. Jadunatah Sinha, *A History of Indian Philosophy*, Calcutta: Sinha Publishing House, 1956, p. 287.

which appear to be out there are really ideas in the mind."[30] Now the question is: whose mind and how many minds? "If an object depends solely on the subject, then, how is it that the mind cannot create at will any object at any time."[31] The dream-metaphor is helpful here: can we dream whatever we want? We can *daydream* whatever we want, but can we dream whatever we want? This would seem to check the slide towards utter subjectivism.

The problem presents itself to both Nisargadatta and Ramaṇa. Here are three passages in which it surfaces in the colloquies of Nisargadatta.

> Q: Do I exist in your world, as you exist in mine?
>
> M: Of course, you are and I am. But only as points in consciousness; we are nothing apart from consciousness. This must be well grasped: the world hangs on the thread of consciousness; no consciousness, no world.
>
> Q: There are many points in consciousness; are there as many worlds?
>
> M: Take dream for an example. In a hospital there may be many patients, all sleeping, all dreaming, each dreaming his own private, personal dream, unrelated, unaffected, having one single factor in common illness. Similarly, we have divorced ourselves in our imagination from the real world of common experience and enclosed ourselves in a cloud of personal desires and fears, images and thoughts, ideas and concepts.
>
> Q: This I can understand. But what could be the cause of the tremendous variety of the personal worlds?
>
> M: The variety is not so great. All the dreams are superimposed over a common world. To some extent they

30. Satischandra Chatterjee and Dhirnedramohan Datta, *op. cit.*, p. 150.

31. *Ibid*, p. 151.

shape and influence each other. The basic unity operates in spite of all. At the root of it all lies self-forgetfulness not knowing who I am.[32]

Q: Well, it is deep mystery to me. I am a simple man.

M: It is you who are deep, complex, mysterious, hard to understand. I am simplicity itself, compared to you. I am what is — without any distinction whatsoever into inner and outer, mine and yours, good and bad. What the world is, I am; what I am the world is.

Q: How does it happen that each man creates his own world?

M: When a number of people are asleep, each dreams his own dream. Only on awakening the question of many different dreams arises and dissolves when they are all seen as dreams, as something imagined.

Q: Even dreams have a foundation.

M: In memory. Even then, what is remembered, is but another dream. The memory of the false cannot but give rise to the false. There is nothing wrong with memory as such. What is false is its content. Remember facts, forget opinions.[33]

Q: Your particular existence and my particular existence, do they both exist in the mind of *Brahman*?

M: The universal is not aware of the particular. The existence as a person is a personal matter. A person exists in time and space, has name and shape, beginning and end; the universal includes all persons, and the absolute is at the root of and beyond all.

---

32. Maurice Frydman, tr., *op. cit.*, pp. 92-93.
33. *Ibid.*, p. 101.

Q: I am not concerned with the totality. My personal consciousness and your personal consciousness - what is the link — between the two?

M: Between two dreamers what can be the link?

Q: They may dream of each other.

M: That is what people are doing. Everyone imagines others and seeks a link with them. The seeker is the link, there is none other.[34]

One may suggest that the configuration of the philosophical idealism of Nisargadatta seems to fit the pattern of the idealistic monism of the *Yogavāśiṣṭha* at the risk of being daring and even potentially in error. Keeping the key and yet controversial nature of the matter under discussion the position of *Yogavāśiṣṭha* may be summarized in this respect. One may point out, however, before doing so, that the dream-metaphor is employed in this text in a manner remarkably reminiscent of both Nisagargadatta and Ramaṇa. Like them according to this text also: "There is thus little difference between the waking and dream experience. Both are alike in their nature as long as each lasts. From the standpoint of a higher Realization, no difference is felt between the two."[35] Nevertheless, on the whole, the paradigm presented in *Yogavāśiṣṭha* seems to provide a closer fit for Nisargadatta. It is summarized below under three headings:

Subjective Idealism

According to the *Yogavāśiṣṭha*, every individual cognizes and perceives only that which is within his own experience; no mind perceives aught but its own ideas. The world experience

---

34. *Ibid.*, p. 256.

35. B.L. Atreya, *op. cit.*, p. 427.

of every individual has arisen individually to every one. Every mind has the power to manufacture its own world.[36]

Objective Idealism

Vasiṣṭha also admits a cosmic world with countless objects and individuals within it, which in its original form is a system of ideas in the cosmic Mind called Brahmā. Brahmā imagines the world and all the individuals within it at the commencement of the creation, and they continue to exist as long as Brahmā lives (III.55.47).[37]

Two Ideals Combined

The ideas imagined by Brahmā (cosmic Mind) are the common objects of experience of us all, although in our own mind they are experienced as our own. It may also be said that they are the reals (*bimba*) which our minds imitate or copy (*pratibimba*). As every mind in itself is an idea of the same cosmic Mind, it is capable of representing within itself other individual minds also as its own ideas. One is an idea in the mind of others as much as others are ideas in that of that one. *As it is possible that several men may see the same dream, it happens that we all experience the same objects.* As the same person may be seen in imagination by many individually, so also the same world-experience is imagined by many individually, so also the same world-experience is imagined in every mind, in the same way as it has arisen in the cosmic Mind.[38]

Ramaṇa's position seems to incline more towards subjective idealism *vis-ā-vis* objective idealism as the following two excerpts indicate which have also been cited earlier: It must be remembered however that the subject in question is not

36. *Ibid.*, p. 428.

37. *Ibid.*

38. *Ibid.*, emphasis added.

the *jīva* but *ātman*, which distinguishes Ramaṇa's position from Buddhist subjective idealism.

> Multiplicity of individuals is a moot point with most persons. A *jīva* is only the light reflected on the ego. The person identifies himself with the ego and argues that there must be more like him. He is not easily convinced of the absurdity of his position. *Does a man who sees many individuals in his dream persist in believing them to be real and enquire after them when he wakes up?*[39]
>
> - - - -
>
> A question was asked why it was wrong to say that there is a multiplicity of *jīvas*. *Jīvas* are certainly many. For a *jīva* is only the ego and forms the reflected light of the Self. Multiplicity of selves may be wrong but not of *jīvas*.
>
> M.: *Jīva* is called so because he sees the world. *A dreamer sees many jīvas in a dream but all of them are not real. The dreamer alone exists and he sees all. So it is with the individual and the world.* There is the creed of only one Self which is also called the creed of only one *jīva*. *It says that the jīva is only one who sees the whole world and the jīvas therein.*
>
> D.: Then *jīva* means the Self here.
>
> M.: So it is. But the Self is not a seer. But here he is said to see the world. So he is differentiated as the *jīva*.[40]

Ramaṇa however seems to maintain that each sees the whole world.

A further limitation of the dream-metaphor, should one choose to regard it as such, springs from the fact that it belongs to the realm of sleep and one might question the applicability of metaphor based on sleep-experience to waking state

---

39. *Talks with Śrī Ramaṇa Maharṣi*, p. 530, emphasis added.

40. *Ibid.*, pp. 530-531, emphasis added.

experience. From this perspective the rope-snake may possess a slight advantage over it. It could be said that:

> So far we have been dealing with the analogy of dream-experience with a view to show that the world of waking also is non-real or illusory. *But illustrations of illusoriness are to be found even in the state of waking*. Just as in the dark a rope which is not determinately known is imagined to be a snake or a streak of water, the self is imagined to be the world through nescience. And, as when the rope is known as rope, the posited snake, etc., vanishes, so also when the self is known as the non-dual reality, the pluralistic world disappears.[41]

This helps identify another limitation of the dream-metaphor as employed in Advaita. Advaita distinguishes the empirical or *vyāvahārika* level of reality from the illusory or *prātibhāsika* level. To make this point the stock examples of a "barren woman's son" and "the hare's horn" are used. Inasmuch as the universe appears "to that extent at any rate" it "cannot be unreal, for the absolutely unreal, like the hare's horn is only words." Ditto for barren woman's son. But what if a barren woman's child appeared in a dream![42]

Yet another limitation of the dream-metaphor in Advaita springs from the fact that if the universe is on a par with the dream, then it should disappear when one wakes up, that is, becomes Realised. But it seems that the universe continues to appear to the Realised being — the difference between the pre- and post-Realization lying in the fact that it is now perceived as part of Brahman rather than apart from it. This leads to the suggestion that the metaphor of the mirage may

---

41. T.M.P. Mahadevan, *Gauḍapāda: A Study in Early Advaita*, p. 128, emphasis added.

42. Edward Conze, ed., *op. cit.*, p. 215.

be more appropriate in such a case, as the mirage continues to appear as such even after it is known to be an illusion. But even the mirage metaphor suffers from a problem — mirage water cannot slake our thirst, but the water drunk by the Realised being in the universe in the post-Realised phase does quench his or her thirst, just as dream water satisfies dream thirst! Thus while in one way the dream-metaphor comes up short, in yet another way it makes up for it. Ramaṇa's remarks of the various metaphors bear recounting here:

> M.: There are different methods of approach to prove the unreality of the universe. The example of the dream is one among many. *Jāgrat, svapna* and *suṣupti* are all treated elaborately in the scripture in order that the Reality underlying them might be revealed. It is not meant to accentuate differences among the three states. The purpose must be kept clearly in view.
>
> Now they say that the world is unreal. Of what degree of unreality is it? Is it like that of a son of a barren mother or a flower in the sky, mere words without any reference to facts? Whereas the world is a fact and not a mere word. The answer is that it is a superimposition on the one Reality, like the appearance of a snake on a coiled rope seen in dim light.
>
> But here too the wrong identity ceases as soon as the friend points out that it is a rope. Whereas in the matter of the world it persists even after it is known to be unreal. How is that? Again the appearance of water in a mirage persists even after the knowledge of mirage is recognized. So it is with the world. Though knowing it to be unreal, it continues to manifest.
>
> But the water of the mirage is not sought to satisfy one's thirst. As soon as one knows that it is a mirage, one gives it up as useless and does not run after it for procuring water.

D.: Not so with the appearance of the world. Even after it is repeatedly declared to be false one cannot avoid satisfying one's wants from the world. How can the world be false?

M.: It is like a man satisfying his dream wants by dream creations. There are objects, there are wants and there is satisfaction. The dream creation is as purposeful as the *jāgrat* world and yet it is not considered real.

Thus we see that each of these illustrations serves a distinct purpose in establishing the stages of unreality. The realised sage finally declares that in the regenerate state the *jāgrat* world also is found to be as unreal as the dream world is found to be in the *jāgrat* state.

Each illustration should be understood in its proper context: it should not be studied as an isolated statement. It is a link in a chain. The purpose of all these is to direct the seeker's mind towards the one Reality underlying them all.[43]

---

43. *Talks with Śri Ramaṇa Maharṣi,* p. 372. Cited earlier in parts.

Bibliography

Atreya, B.L., 1954, *Yogavāsiṣṭha and Modern Thought*, Banaras: The Indian Book Shop.

———, 1953, "Philosophy of the *Yogavāsiṣṭha*," in *The Cultural Heritage of India*, Haridas Bhattacharyya, editor, Calcutta (Kolkata): The Ramakrishna Mission Institute of Culture, vol. III. pp. 424-36.

Balsubramaniam, R., 1976, *Advaita Vedānta*, Madras (Chennai): University of Madras.

Brandon, S.G.F., ed., 1970, *A Dictionary of Comparative Religion*. New York: Macmillan Publishing Company.

Brunton, Paul and Venkatramiah, Mudagala, 1984, *Conscious Immortality*. Tiruvannāmalai: Sri Ramanāsramam.

Campbell, Joseph, 1974, *The Mythic Image*, Princeton: Princeton University Press.

Cenkner, William, 1983, *A Tradition of Teachers: Śaṅkara and the Jagadgurus Today*, Delhi: Motilal Banarsidass.

Chatterjee, Satischandra and Datta, Dhirendramohan, 1950, *An Introduction to Indian Philosophy*, Calcutta (Kolkata): University of Calcutta.

Conze, Edward, 1959, *Buddhism: Its Essence and Development*, New York: Harper & Row.

———, *et al.*, eds., 1954, *Buddhist Texts Through the Ages*, New York: Philosophical Library.

Cornford, Francis Macdonald, 1956, *Plato's Cosmology*, London: Routledge & Kegan Paul.

———, tr., 1955, *The Republic of Plato*, Oxford: Clarendon Press.

Craven, Roy C., 1976, *A Concise History of Indian Art*, London: Thames & Hudson.

Crombie, I.M., 1962, *An Examination of Plato's Doctrines*, New York: Routledge & Kegan Paul, vol. I.

Dasgupta, Surendranath, 1951, *A History of Indian Philosophy,* Cambridge: Cambridge University Press.

De Bary, Wm. Theodore, *et al.*, 1960, *Sources of Chinese Tradition,* New York: Columbia University Press.

Descartes, Rene, 1972, *Discourse on Method and the Meditations,* tr., P.E. Sutcliffe. Harmondsworth: Penguin Books.

Deutsch, Eliot and Van Buitenen, J.A.B., eds., 1971, *A Source Book of Advaita Vedānta,* Honolulu: The University Press of Hawaii.

Deutsch, Eliot, 1969, *Advaita Vedānta: A Philosophical Reconstruction,* Honolulu: East-West Center Press.

O'Flaherty, Wendy Doniger, 1984, *Dreams, Illusion and Other Realities.* Chicago and London: The University of Chicago Press.

Dunn, Jean, ed., 1982, *Seeds of Consciousness: The Wisdom of Śrī Nisargadatta Maharāj,* New York: Grove Press Inc.

Faraday, Ann, 1980, *Dream Power,* New York: Berkeley Books.

Frydman, Maurice, tr., 1973, *I Am That: Conversations With Śrī Nisargadatta Maharāj,* Bombay (Mumbai): Chetana.

Gambhirananda, Swami, tr., 1965, *Brahma-sūtra-bhāṣya of Śrī Śaṅkarācārya,* Calcutta (Kolkata): Advaita Ashrama.

Goodman, David, ed., 1985, *The Teachings of Śrī Ramaṇa Maharṣi,* New York: Arkana.

Green, Celia, 1968, *Lucid Dreams,* Oxford: Institute of Psychophysical Research.

Grimes, John, 2004, *The Vivekacūḍāmaṇi of Śaṅkarācārya Bhagavatpāda,* Hants, England: Ashgate Publishing Company.

Hiriyanna, M., 1948, *The Essentials of Indian Philosophy,* London: George Allen & Unwin.

———, 1983, *Outlines of Indian Philosophy.* Bombay (Mumbai): Blackie & Son Publishers Private Limited.

Hume, Robert Ernest, tr., 1968, *The Thirteen Principal Upaniṣads,* second edition, revised, London: Oxford University Press.

Indich, William E., 1980, *Consciousness in Advaita Vedānta,* Delhi: Motilal Banarsidass.

Jacobi, Jolande, 1959, *Complex Archetype Symbol in the Psychology of C.G. Jung,* Princeton: Princeton University Press.

Kilborne, Benjamin, 1987, "Dreams," in *The Encyclopedia of Religion*, editor in chief, Mircea Eliade, New York: Macmillan Publishing Company, vol. 4.

Long, Bruce, 1987, "Underworld," in *The Encyclopedia of Religion*, Mircea Eliade, editor-in-chief, New York: The Macmillan Press, vol. 15.

Madhavananda, Swami, tr., 1966, *Vivekacūdāmaṇi of Śrī Śaṅkaracārya*, Calcutta (Kolkata): Advaita Ashram.

Mahadevan, T.M.P., 1960, *Gauḍapāda: A Study in Early Advaita*, Madras (Chennai): University of Madras.

———, 1971, *Outlines of Hinduism*, Bombay (Mumbai): Chetana Limited.

Malalalsekara, G.P., ed., *Encyclopaedia of Buddhism*, Colombo: Government of Ceylon (Sri Lanka).

Mani, Vettam, 1975, *Purāṇic Encyclopaedia*. Delhi: Motilal Banarsidass.

Manusmṛti.

Manser, A.R., 1967, "Dreams," in *The Encyclopedia of Philosophy*, Paul Edwards, editor in chief, New York: The Macmillan Company and the Free Press. vol. II.

Mārkaṇḍeya Purāṇa.

Mitra, Vihari Lal, 1998, *The Yoga-vāsiṣṭha of Vālmīki*, Delhi: Parimal Publications. Four volumes.

Mudaliar, A. Devaraja, 1978, *Gems From Bhagavan*, Tiruvannāmalai: Śrī Ramanāsramam.

Murty, K. Satchidananda, 1974, *Revelation and Reason in Advaita Vedānta*, Delhi: Motilal Banarsidass.

Osborne, Arthur, 1995, *Ramaṇa Maharṣi and the Path of Self-Knowledge*, York Beach, Maine: Samuel Weiser, Inc.

———, ed., 1971, *The Teachings of Bhagavan Śrī Ramaṇa Maharṣi in His Own Words*, Tiruvannāmalai: Śrī Ramanāsramam.

Radhakrishnan, S., ed., 1953, *The Principal Upaniḍads*. London: George Allen & Unwin.

———, tr., 1960, *The Brahma-Sūtra*. London: George Allen & Unwin Ltd.

Rajeswarananda, Swami, 1974, *Erase the Ego*, Bombay (Mumbai): Bharatiya Vidya Bhavan.

Rajneesh, Bhagwan Shree, 1972, *I Am the Gate*, Bombay (Mumbai): Life Awakening Center.

Raju, P.T., 1953, *Idealistic Thought in India*, London: George Allen & Unwin.

———, 1937, "Indian Philosophy," in *The Cultural Heritage of India*, Haridas Bhattacharyya, editor, Calcutta (Kolkata): The Ramakrishna Mission Institute of Culture.

Renou, Louis, ed., 1962, *Hinduism*, New York: George Braziller.

Reps, Paul, compiler, 1961, *Zen Flesh, Zen Bones*, New York: Doubleday & Company Ltd.

Rushdie, Salman, 1988, *The Satanic Verses*. New York: Viking Penguin Inc.

Sambuddhananda, Swami, 1959, *Vedānta Through Stories*, Bombay (Mumbai): Sri Ramakrishna Ashram.

Sankaranarayanan, P., 1970, *What Is Advaita?*, Bombay (Mumbai): Bharatiya Vidya Bhavan.

Sarasvathī, Swāmī Śrī Ramaṇānanda, tr., 1980, *Tripurā Rahasya or the Mystery Beyond the Trinity*, Tiruvannāmalai: Śrī Ramaṇāśramam.

Sharma, Arvind, 1986, "The Significance of Viṣṇu Reclining on the Serpent," *Religion* 16: pp. 101-14.

Sharma, Chandradhar, 1960, *A Critical Survey of Indian Philosophy*, London: Rider & Co.

Sinha, Jadunath, 1956, *A History of Indian Philosophy*, Calcutta (Kolkata): Sinha Publishing House.

———, 1958, *Indian Psychology: Cognition*, Calcutta (Kolkata): Sinha Publishing House.

Swami, B.V. Narasimha, 1985, *Self-Realization: The Life and Teachings of Śrī Ramaṇa Maharṣi*, Tiruvannāmali: Śrī Ramaṇāśramam.

Talks With Śrī Ramaṇa Maharṣi, 1984, Tiruvannamalai: Śrī Ramaṇāśramam.

Venkatesananda, Swami, 1984, *The Concise Yoga Vāsiṣṭha*, Albany, NY: State University of New York Press.

Viṣṇu Purāṇa

Walsh, W.H., 1967, "Immanuel Kant," in *The Encyclopaedia of Philosophy*, Paul Edwards, editor in chief, New York: The Macmillan Company and the Free Press, vol. IV.

Zimmer, Heinrich, 1962, *Myths and Symbols in Indian Art and Civilization*. Edited by Joseph Campbell. New York: Harper & Row.

———, 1951, *Philosophies of India*, Edited by Joseph Campbell. New York: Pantheon Books.

Author Index

Subject Index